SUPPOSE WE LET CIVILIZATION BEGIN

by

Richard W. Wetherill

HUMANETICS FELLOWSHIP™

COPYRIGHT © 1978, 1979, 1991
BY
HUMANETICS FELLOWSHIP
ROYERSFORD, PA 19468

All Rights Reserved

PRINTED IN THE UNITED STATES OF AMERICA

Contents

PREFACE TO PART I	1
PART I—THE BASIC FLAW	3
UNREASONING INTERFERENCE	4
HIDDEN MOTIVES	5
POWER OF MOTIVES	7
CONTROL BY MOTIVES	8
ORDINARY HONESTY	10
HIDDEN DANGER	11
INHERITED MISTAKES	12
CAUSE OF THE FLAW	14
THE SERIOUS THREAT	15
SYSTEMS OF REASONING	17
THE SUBTLE TRAP	18
PREFACE TO PART II	21
PART II—THE BASIC LAW	23
UNREFUTED EVIDENCE	24
UNDERLYING PRINCIPLES	26
COUNTERFEIT PRINCIPLES	38
IRRATIONALITY	39
GENUINE PRINCIPLES	31
RATIONALITY	33
LIFE WITHOUT FEAR	35
UNSCIENTIFIC THINKING	36
SCIENTIFIC THINKING	37
INTELLIGENCE	39

PREFACE TO PART III 43

PART III—THE BASIC PLAN 45

    ESCAPE FROM TROUBLE 46
    SUPPOSITIONAL REASONING 48
    THE DANGER OF BELIEVING 50
    WHAT CONSTITUTES PROOF 51
    THE LOGIC OF REALITY 53
    ACCESSIBILITY OF INFORMATION 55
    ADOPTION OF HONESTY 56
    OBVIOUS EVIDENCE 59
    THE ASTONISHING RELEASE 61

CONCLUSION: EVIDENCE OF THINGS NOT SEEN 65

ADVENTURES IN HUMANETICS 69

INTRODUCTION TO EXPERIENTIAL MATERIAL 71

    STOPPING FAMILY FIGHTS 75
    THE DEVIL MADE ME DO IT 96
    RELATIONSHIPS 98
    GAMES 124

Preface to Part I

BY APPLYING what is said in this section, the members of a group of young people stopped their involvement in typical teenage trouble over smoking, drinking, drugs, and sex. The changes came one by one, but each change was sudden and effortless and proved to be lasting.

Preteen children also reduced their misbehavior sufficiently that they no longer needed scoldings or punishments. Instead, calling their attention to misbehavior proved sufficient to end it because the kids themselves had determined that they should behave themselves in a civilized manner.

Parents and school authorities were delighted.

Numerous adults adopted and applied the same information in their vocational and private lives and ended their arguments. Anyone who thoughtfully and honestly considers all the details presently is able to understand why.

At first some of the information may seem too good to be true—but that condition passes as soon as the information is fully and correctly understood.

Part I

The Basic Flaw

A VERY simple flaw has kept people locked in multitudinous kinds of trouble. That flaw is causing conflicts, accidents, sicknesses, compulsions, bad habits, personality faults of all kinds.

It is causing people to lose their lives—to kill themselves and each other—needlessly.

It is a flaw of thinking, a flaw expressed in conversation, a flaw that causes irrational behavior. It is a congenital flaw, a flaw with which everyone is afflicted. It is a flaw that is reinforced by the thinking and behavior of parents, older brothers and sisters, teachers, clergymen, people in every category of life without their awareness.

The reason this presentation is deemed practical at the present time is that a modest number of persons have demonstrated that they have achieved a reasonably clear, correct understanding of the flaw. They have made substantial progress toward counteracting and eliminating its influence. As a consequence, some very great improvements have developed in their lives. Improvements are still developing.

People of mature years, young people, even small children have produced the evidence. As a spectacular example, those children have made it clear that recognizing and giving attention to that flaw makes every kind of disciplinary action unnecessary. Instead of the former disciplinary action, the kids call each other's attention to behavior that is not satisfactory. They refuse to support each other's wrong behavior, want no support for their own, and accept suggestions with good grace.

Unreasoning Interference

MORE THAN fifty years of careful research were needed to surmount initial resistance to information about the flaw, because the flaw itself tended to cause numerous misunderstandings.

Because of it, the information was hotly resented, lied about, discredited, evaded, counteracted, and contradicted by almost everybody. Very few wanted to hear one word about it. Oddly, the most vigorous opposition came from those precise persons who had the greatest obligation to study closely and carefully the information that described the flaw. Had they done so, many years of confusion, trouble and turmoil could have been avoided to society's lasting benefit.

It is not known whether the influential persons in the fields of education, government, industry, commerce, religion, family life, and elsewhere are ready to look with honesty—which is all it takes—at a description of the flaw. But those persons who are willing to look with honesty at that description will find it extremely helpful. They can achieve the kind of lives they have always wanted but have never been able to achieve.

They can replace turmoil, conflict, struggle, and various disastrous results that have developed in their lives with life as it should be—as it demonstrably is for those persons who clearly and correctly understand the flaw.

The Basic Flaw

Most persons can easily observe that a child is born with the inclination to get his own way. He takes what he wants with no concern for who owns it. In later life that is regarded as dishonest, but the infant is presumed innocent, and his action is commonly overlooked.

At a certain stage, a person wants to be known as a law-abiding citizen and may scrupulously try to avoid taking anything that does not belong to him. But a small child goes through stages in which he unhesitatingly takes whatever he wants just because he keeps trying to get his own way.

As a child grows older, in all probability, he may go through a pilfering stage in which he steals money from his mother's purse or at least cookies from the pantry, fruit from the refrigerator, even candy or cigarettes from a store.

Hidden Motives

CHILDREN ARE easily excused for dishonest behavior largely because parents remember what they did at a similar age. But a part of the process of achieving such degrees of civilization as exist have been achieved by the development of some understanding of the concept that stealing is wrong.

Relatively little has been accomplished by that understanding. It is immediately obvious that a society that requires laws and penalties against stealing must be a dishonest society.

Ours is a dishonest society. Ours is such an outrageously uncivilized society that we even need laws against murder. That fact by itself should prove that civilization has not yet developed.

Murder is not thought of as stealing. But it is. It deprives another person of his life. Murder is usually not thought of as an act of dishonesty. But it is. It is preceded by dishonesty in the form of stealth and concealment of weapons; conducted in dishonesty by care exerted to avoid observation, detection and later arrest; then followed by dishonesty in the form of pretense that the murder was not committed and by outright denial of guilt.

The basic flaw is dishonesty.

Each person expresses inborn dishonesty. The average person takes what he wants and says anything he thinks will get the result he wants. He is not concerned about whether he is honest. He is just concerned about whether he can manage to get his own way.

Of course many persons deny that. They assert that they try hard to be honest. But if they look at the facts carefully enough, they discover that they are not really trying to be honest. Rather, they are trying hard to avoid the penalties of dishonesty. They are trying not to get caught and branded as liars or thieves. Rather, they are trying to avoid jail terms. Some are trying to stay out of hell and get into heaven.

There is always a motive other than the motive to be honest although research shows that it is often subtly hidden.

Perhaps the most vigorous of all the denials that have come to my attention have come from religious persons. In the heat of their denials, they have quoted scripture by remarks such as, "The Bible says there's nothing new under the sun!" True, it does. But it also says, "Behold, I make all things new."

In an astonishing variety of ways, lies, outright lies, have been used by those people to contradict, discredit and oppose the importance of adopting absolute honesty as a way of life.

Some religious groups teach that children are not responsible, that they are innocent, that they do not know right from wrong until age seven or eight. But children younger than six have testified to the contrary. Every child who understands the information presented here testified that he knew right from wrong. Because of their recognition of personal responsibility, those children have been able to make an exciting escape from the consequences of their dishonesty and from the dishonesty itself. Results go far beyond what people are likely to expect.

Not only has opposition come from religious persons, but it has also come from scientific thinkers. Some of them have become so eager to discredit the information that they were willing to assert that the sum of two plus two does not always equal four—and vehemently insist on the point.

Power of Motives

ON VARIOUS occasions I have stood in front of an audience with two silver dollars in my right hand and two silver dollars in my left hand, placed one pair on top of the other, and then counted four showing that two and two do equal four. I have offered any doubter a chance to take the four silver dollars and add two plus two and get five or five thousand. I have offered the extra dollars as a reward for any person who could do it. For obvious reasons never was there a taker. It is not possible to add two plus two correctly and get anything but four. No more, no less. If it were, it would obviously be possible with silver dollars.

That demonstration never changed the thinking of the dishonest person. The reason is that what people say is determined by their motives. They refuse to say what puts them in the position of contradicting their motives, and that is something they do not, at first, know about themselves.

Despite the foregoing, there exists what might be

described as a decent sector of society wherein people do try to be honest. They try to tell the truth. They try to avoid stealing. In a variety of other ways, they attempt to practice the principles of honesty. They have been taught to do so in their families, their churches and schools.

The result is what commonly passes for honesty in our society, but it is only a fraction of what is needed to constitute absolute honesty. It is a kind of superficial honesty achieved not for the sake of honesty itself, but because people assume they will be happier and get into less trouble with the persons who deal with them. Some people assume they will have a better chance of getting a heavenly reward.

Honesty for the sake of a reward is not true honesty. The proof of honesty comes when a person is honest because it is the right way to behave.

When a person analyzes the difference between what he says and what is the literal truth, he gets many shocks, especially when discussing his motives. When he puts attention on his motives as best he understands them, he is surprised to discover that he hides many of them, falsifies them as a means of hiding them and does everything he can to avoid exposing them. Thus he discovers that he is not absolutely honest about what he tells people in many of his ordinary conversations.

Control by Motives

WHEN A person thinks carefully enough about the details of his ordinary conversation, he discovers that in virtually everything he says he ordinarily gives expression to one factor only: whatever enables him to make the impression he wants to make.

The Basic Flaw

He rarely considers the factuality and correctness of his remarks except insofar as he thinks factuality and correctness would help him to get the result he wants. His attention is on trying to make a favorable impression and avoid, if possible, any unfavorable impressions.

When people notice someone's irrational conversation, they rarely consider it dishonest. They may regard it as slipshod or as rationalizing, but usually they do not define it. Sometimes they are too busy talking the same way themselves.

What passes for honesty in our society will be seen to be very superficial compared with the real thing.

The reality about dishonesty cannot be discerned by a person who does not closely and honestly inspect his conversation, his behavior and especially his thinking. If he is fully honest, he discovers that he departs from reality in various ways many times. He may do it repeatedly in his patterns of thinking, conversation and behavior.

That was such unpopular information originally that scores of techniques were devised as a means of getting around the obstacles in people's thinking and inducing them to make experiments. Ultimately those experiments had the effect of changing people's approach to life so that the extent of their dishonesty gradually became clear.

Although members of our research group had originally resented statements suggesting that they had dishonest inclinations, they gradually became aware that the greatest proportion of their dishonesty had a way of expressing itself without their awareness.

During one phase of preparatory work several decades ago, the term unconscious dishonesty was used as a means of penetrating the block. Success was delayed for two prominent reasons among others. One reason is that people resented being told they were dishonest under any circumstance in any situation of life, even when given the relief of knowing they did not intend the dishonesty. The other is that people could not detect unconscious dishonesty simply because it was indeed unconscious. Consequently, at first, they were not able to recognize the convincing evidence for themselves.

Since that time, many persons have observed the evidence. Instead of resisting and resenting the information, they feel a sensation of relief and release. In addition, they acquired the ability to eliminate every kind of dishonesty made conscious, recognized and correctly understood. As a consequence, they no longer issue a stream of invitations to confusion, accidents, sicknesses, conflicts, problems, troubles, and disasters of a variety of different kinds as formerly when those elements of unconscious dishonesty were not detected nor recognized nor correctly understood.

Ordinary Honesty

IT HAS now been demonstrated that such detection, recognition and understanding can become the prelude to a kind of life improvement that was previously considered impossible. It is a kind of improvement that is correctly described as the development of a new and better personality and a new plan of life that includes successful relationships and right opportunities.

That, however, requires more than ordinary honesty.

Even ordinary honesty is not universal. We read that merchants suffer enormous losses because of shoplifting, that employers suffer enormous losses because of stealing and advantage taking, that our relief system is overloaded with dishonest practices. Insurance costs have skyrocketed because of false or exaggerated claims. The deficit is out of bounds because of the inclination of people in every segment of society to take advantage in any conceivable way. One clear consequence is an inflated economy that amounts to wholesale theft. The value of savings leaks out of savings accounts, safe-deposit boxes, investments and whatever money people have in their purses and wallets. Somebody else gets the value, and that is what constitutes the theft.

Hidden Danger

CLEAR UNDERSTANDING of the breadth and depth of dishonesty in society is shocking to everybody who sees a tenth of it. When that shock is multiplied by ten, it is seen that ***dishonesty on an unimagined scale has been incorporated into society's way of life.*** But people's attention has been diverted from that reality by concern that they would not be able to act on their urges—the precise urges causing the unconscious dishonesty.

Hidden danger results not from people's failure to avoid obvious dishonesty but their failure to understand dishonesty in all its forms. People are hesitant about telling lies when they know they are lying. Yet they tell lie after lie after lie without the awareness they are lying. They do it when they misrepresent their motives and their thinking. They do it when they say what they think will get results they want without regard for correctness.

The average person is also confused about stealing.

When people avoid actually taking what does not belong to them, they avoid only a small part of the stealing that is rampant. They demand pay raises to which they are not entitled, thus contributing to inflation; impose needlessly on other people's time and attention; push ahead of people waiting in line. Very few think of that commonplace activity as stealing, although an honest person sees that it is.

Obviously many people have limited awareness of the full nature of both lying and stealing.

Beyond the concepts of ordinary dishonesty is a concept of honesty that transcends both conscious and unconscious dishonesty. Experimenters who have done the work leading to these findings characteristically refer to it as absolute honesty—and more commonly as absolute right.

Quite possibly the concept of absolute right has been argued against, ridiculed, discredited, and rejected even more rigorously than has the notion that people are universally dishonest. But the concept of absolute right represents the reality of the kind of honesty that should be achieved. It is demonstrated that failure to achieve it causes the flaws in people's thinking that make them irrational, puts them out of touch with reality, and causes them to issue a large proportion of all their routine invitations to trouble of all kinds.

Inherited Mistakes

EVEN THE children who successfully applied the pertinent information have demonstrated that the failures, problems and fears of ordinary life diminish in direct proportion to the success achieved in making the changes that result from adoption of absolute honesty.

The reason for that needs to be understood.

Each generation has contributed its share to the perpetuation of the sad state of affairs that exists. That state is one in which not only is each person born with dishonest tendencies, but in carrying the burden of providing education for children, the older generation has lacked the knowledge and

The Basic Flaw

inclination to remedy matters by raising the level of honesty. Parents, teachers and others responsible for the education of children have seen no reason why they should attempt to raise children's honesty above the level of their own.

Under analysis the reason for that oversight is clear.

How could a parent or teacher enable a child to overcome inclinations to express unconscious dishonesty when neither the parent nor the teacher ever learned to detect unconscious dishonesty in himself? The fact that no generation espoused absolute honesty has kept a restrictive ceiling over the level of honesty achievable by any generation. But now, a small segment of the present generation is demonstrating that it has overcome the problem of penetrating that restrictive ceiling.

If there has never been an honest generation, at least, one is getting started. That statement might seem like an exaggeration to a person who has not seen the evidence. Very possibly he might brand the statement as false, but only because of his dishonesty whether he is aware of it or not.

People's opposition and resentment often cause them to display irresponsibility.

It is an act of irresponsibility to deny any statement without the ability to support the denial. It is an act of dishonesty to refuse to look at the evidence that supports a statement while denying the validity of the statement. It is an act of dishonesty to dissuade other persons from participating in a program that is based on obviously correct information. Those and other misleading acts of dishonesty were performed by persons who will change when they understand.

Cause of the Flaw

WHETHER CONSCIOUS or unconscious, dishonesty has blighted the intelligence of the very persons who should have strongest inclination to look directly at the reality and determine what statements flow out of that reality.

That puts attention on the precise description of the nature of the flaw with which a person is born.

Not enough description of that flaw is provided by a statement that people are born dishonest. A more illuminating statement is needed. Perhaps one found in the description of a specific situation in which they display dishonesty.

The flaw is expressed in what could correctly be described as a person's wrong approach to life.

The reality is that ordinarily nobody has the conscious intent to be dishonest. He does not purposely adopt the intent to steal or lie or to take advantage. He just has the intent to get his own way by acting on his urges and the way he feels. That makes him act on the inclinations that arise from his motives and urges whether they are conscious or unconscious.

His driving force is not a motive to be dishonest but simply a motive to get his own way.

During situation after situation, he is frustrated in his efforts to get his own way. He reacts emotionally to the frustration and thinks, says and does something wrong. But whether he is frustrated or is merely proceeding in an unhindered manner to get his own way, his real intent is to do whatever he wants to do. And in his conversation, his real intent is to say whatever he wants to say.

He rarely sees any reason to consider whether he is honest or not. As an infant, he cannot know the difference between honesty and dishonesty. He needs to learn it, but each older generation has made the mistake of teaching only that kind of honesty it understands and only as much as the older generation wants to teach. It is not comprehensive: Parents often ask their children to make untruthful statements to avoid embarrassment for the parents.

The Serious Threat

PARENTS TEACH only the portion of honesty that they approve of and understand. If they do not know about unconscious dishonesty, they are unable to teach it. The experimenters discovered that the damage done by unconscious dishonesty is vastly more extensive than the damage done by conscious dishonesty.

Conscious dishonesty gets children scolded and punished at home and at school. It gets adults arrested, jailed and worse. But unconscious dishonesty is far more rampant. It expresses itself many times oftener than conscious dishonesty because it flows out of unconscious motives that ordinarily cannot be detected. For that reason the danger of unconscious dishonesty has gone unrecognized.

It is consistently concealed behind a wall of fear lest it be exposed. It is often used to justify various kinds of action that any thoughtful person readily recognizes as wrong. It has caused people to refuse to receive and consider the information that would enable them to see the reality.

The inclination of the individual to get his own way, at first glance, need not be regarded as dishonest. It need only be recognized as the reality. Then, under analysis, the desire for one's way is seen as an inclination that has to depend on dishonesty for gratification. The inclination diverts attention away from considerations of right and wrong, ignoring consideration of dishonesty, because it directs attention toward efforts to satisfy the inclination.

The result is carelessness about thinking.

While a person is careless about his thinking, he can successfully disregard his lying, cheating, stealing, taking advantage, and other dishonest practices. He can successfully disregard the fact that he is falsifying his thinking and conversation, misrepresenting his behavior and concealing his true motives. He can habitually engage in those performances as a way of life without ever becoming aware of his dishonesty until he develops the willingness to look at the reality of what is happening.

When a person does look, he makes many astonishing discoveries. One of those discoveries is that in teaching honesty and avoidance of dishonesty to children, successive generations of parents have confronted their children with an impossible contradiction that cannot be resolved until the dishonesty is recognized and dropped.

Each generation has taught children to adopt motives, seek advantages and to behave in ways that are given respectful consideration by society. Such action cannot be carried out without dishonesty.

Parents admonish their children to be honest, while at the same time, they teach behavior patterns that require dishonesty. In that way they confront the rising generation with behavioral requirements that are unrealistic and cannot be met. The parents are in the position of expecting children honestly to engage in a dishonest way of life.

Few persons have honestly considered the contradictory pattern just described.

In the beginning a careful person sees the evidence that such is the pattern. He may think he has seen it all when, in fact, he sees just a tiny piece. As he extends his areas of observation, he gets shock after shock after shock. That process goes on during a period of continuing shocks as he sees how many respected performances of public and private life actually depend on dishonesty for their accomplishment.

Systems of Reasoning

AS UNDERSTANDING grows, an entirely new pattern of thinking becomes observable. Those persons who have done the successful experimenting have seen the new pattern. Having seen that, they are able to recognize and understand the old pattern. They become aware that ***two diametrically opposite systems of reasoning are available to the general public.*** One of those systems is dishonest, and it forces people to make a more or less constant effort to be honest. But only the dishonesty of the dishonest system necessitates their effort to be honest, and the dishonesty often frustrates that effort.

In a subtle way, any resulting honesty becomes just an expression of unconscious dishonesty.

That is a concept that may be difficult for a person to understand until after he has gained understanding of both systems of reasoning. He is helped when he realizes that no person need try to be honest unless he is tempted to be dishonest. Also when he realizes that honesty is sometimes used as a tool to achieve a dishonest purpose.

From the foregoing, it becomes evident that honesty as a policy cannot be genuine honesty. Rather it is a counterfeit procedure used to get an advantage. But advantage itself is dishonest, for the simple reason that a person cannot get an advantage except by disadvantaging at least one other person.

That suggests a kind of unnoticed dishonesty that is rampant everywhere in human affairs.

On the surface it might seem that the ordinary system of reasoning could be called a system of honesty because the better portion of society lives in that system and does try to be honest. But that effort is needed only because of the dishonesty that is inherent in the system.

The really basic distinction is not adequately described in terms of honesty and dishonesty. It is better described by the names of the two systems commonly used by the experimenters who helped in the research: the relative system of reasoning and the absolute system of reasoning.

The Subtle Trap

EACH PERSON is born into the relative system in which a person spends his life trying to act on his urges. Consequently he tends to be indiscriminate about both honesty and dishonesty in ways he does not suspect. He seldom tries to be honest or dishonest. He merely tries to get his own way. If he thinks honesty will get it, he tends to be honest. If he thinks dishonesty will get it, he tends to be dishonest. Except on rare occasions, he fails to notice either the honesty or the dishonesty.

What is wrong with the system is that it keeps his attention on his urges to get his own way and diverts his attention from the reality of his predicament. When he changes his system of reasoning, his urges lose their hold on his mind.

The absolute system of reasoning is to be regarded as neither an honest system nor a dishonest system. It is a system in which a person need not attempt to be honest because there is no dishonesty in the system.

Honesty and dishonesty become irrelevant in the absolute system, because in that system, a person does not reason

The Basic Flaw

from his urges based on contradictory motives. Instead, he reasons from reality, and he does not try to get his own way. Instead, he tries to take whatever action is called for by the reality of whatever is happening.

He cannot do that if he falsifies reality in his thoughts.

If he successfully falsifies reality to himself, he becomes irrational because he loses touch with reality. In addition if he successfully falsifies reality to others, they may take irrational action because they believe his falsification.

When a person reasons from his motives, his urges, his likes and dislikes, his attention is not on reality. That is exactly what is wrong with the relative system of reasoning: It separates a person from whatever reality he disregards. Consequently he makes unrealistic decisions that cannot work satisfactorily. They invite trouble.

Because he fails to understand the two systems, he fails to realize that his disregard for reality is responsible for his trouble. He fails to realize that he has brought the trouble on himself, so he tends to blame it on other people or on conditions outside himself. Therefore, he cannot eliminate it.

When he learns to reason from reality, his troubles reduce. His behavioral problems become solvable and can be eliminated. His conflicts diminish.

Of course, that is not what he expects in the beginning. Instead, he is afraid. He fears that his past misdeeds will be discovered and bring him disgrace. But honesty does not require that a person expose his secrets. In a dishonest world, exposing secrets invites additional trouble.

Things are different in the absolute system.

The record shows that people in the absolute system achieve a kind of satisfaction and success formerly unattainable. It is true that each person is figuratively caught with his hand in the cookie jar, but it is also true that all the others know he is reformed. ***The result is a new kind of freedom in which nobody holds anything against anybody.***

THE PERSON who feels an inclination to deny or refute what is said in this section demonstrates his pressing need for the information. He may not recognize his need, but the persons who understand the information recognize it.

They know he needs information about himself, and about his unconscious motives. Perhaps also about whatever group he may represent.

Every objection to the information has come from a person who failed to see the reality behind the information. That reality is convincing.

It discloses many attractive opportunities.

Many persons who formerly objected to the information decided to take another look, saw what they had missed and changed their minds. A typical comment from those persons is this: "When a person gets correct understanding, he suddenly does an about-face. After that, he can't not start making constructive changes in his life!"

Preface to Part II

WHAT IS said in this section will increase the productivity and effectiveness of every person or group of persons who study and apply the information. That has been shown by persons from many walks of life, of virtually all ages and various degrees of education and experience.

The information already has a long history.

It was formalized forty years ago after more than twenty years of incubation. It developed into an extremely complicated and ramified body of knowledge that, at last, is reduced to certain essentials readily comprehensible by any person who devotes honest attention to it.

Even small children now show comprehension.

Getting the information understood by small children involved a procedure of teaching first the grandparents, then the parents, then a group of sons and daughters who taught still younger kids and continued down the line until the information was received by preschool children.

From that work, an improved life has emerged.

Part II

The Basic Law

THREE DISTINCT kinds of laws influence the behavior of people. In this section they are designated as ***man-made, self-made, and natural or God-made laws.*** Experience shows that the persons who get understanding of all three kinds make spectacular improvements in their lives.

They discover the basic cause of trouble.

That enables a person to change his approach to life in ways that let him avoid innumerable kinds of ordinary distress. It enables him to end a multitude of burdensome problems that he had thought were a necessary part of life. It enables him to find and establish a safe plan of life in which things tend to work out satisfactorily for everybody.

At first those statements may seem exaggerated, but they are no exaggeration to the persons who correctly understand all three kinds of laws mentioned above.

They know that the understanding has important uses.

They watched quarrels, arguments, disagreements and conflicts diminish and disappear from their lives. They watched young people suddenly stop their trouble over smoking, drinking, drugs, sex, vandalism and shoplifting. They watched adults make astonishing improvements in their personal and vocational lives. They watched small children achieve behavioral improvements that virtually eliminated the necessity for discipline by scoldings and punishments from teachers and parents.

For each person who gains correct understanding, those improvements are the norm. Any person who devotes really careful attention to the details until he understands them then knows that the foregoing statements are indeed correct.

Unrefuted Evidence

HE DISCOVERS that many kinds of trouble result from his being guided by the wrong laws.

He does not have to accept that information on faith or because it is stated by someone in authority. He sees the reality himself. He gladly acts in accord with that reality because he sees it as the way out of trouble he could not formerly avoid.

He understands exactly why the information was initially evaded and suppressed and why it seemed offensive at first. He becomes aware that only misunderstandings made it seem offensive. He recognizes it as a way of getting mental and emotional relief and release.

He also learns about a sound approach to safe learning.

HE GETS his information from the printed page, but that is not what provides real understanding. At first he cannot be sure whether the information is correct. If he judges it or accepts a judgment from someone else, he just substitutes the judgment for the information. Judgments are not reliable.

He should look carefully at the reality to which the information points. That approach is what brings understanding because reality constitutes the natural source of evidence that cannot honestly be refuted.

In effect, a person who looks at the reality is learning from the book of life. He is getting safe information because he is learning in precisely the same way as he earlier learned about black and white, up and down, big and little, night and day.

The Basic Law

Nobody could possibly convince him that black is white, up is down, big is little, or night is day because he has direct knowledge of the evidence. The information is safe because he has seen the reality.

A person learns about man-made laws from other people. Those laws are often disagreeable.

They come from parents: "Don't touch!" They come from teachers: "Be quiet!" They come from strangers: "Look out!" They also come from clubs, unions, employers, churches and governments.

The same person must think carefully to learn about self-made laws. They arise inside his mind: "I'll do as I please!" If he thinks about how they work, he can see that he must enforce them himself, although man-made laws are enforced by others. He may also see that neither man-made laws nor self-made laws are either fully rational or genuinely reliable.

The fact is that natural laws are both rational and reliable.

A person learns about natural laws without realizing that he is learning about them early in life. For example, consider how a toddler learns about gravity by falling and getting bumped.

People learn that natural laws are special.

They may disobey man-made laws. They may struggle desperately to enforce self-made laws. But they are helpless in the grip of natural laws. They are compelled to live or die by those laws, and that is why people show great respect for gravity.

Consider how children try to balance when learning to walk. Consider how carefully adults move on a slippery surface. Consider how everybody struggles to regain his balance the instant he has lost it.

Their actions show people's respect for the law of gravity.

They have similar respect for every natural law they recognize. They carefully avoid trouble with heat, electricity, poisons and approaching vehicles.

A person literally cannot disobey a natural law. Even while falling to his death because he failed to keep his balance, he goes on obeying the law of gravity.

Underlying Principles

A PERSON shows respect for natural laws because there is no other way he can avoid the trouble that results when he disregards them.

By allowing for them properly, he is safe.

He does not get burned, shocked, poisoned, or bumped unless he lets himself be negligent about some natural law. If he is negligent, the outcome is the same for him as for anybody else. Natural laws make no concession for his ignorance, innocence, education, intelligence, religion or anything else.

Despite those facts, people cause themselves trouble by making two common mistakes.

First, a person may have his attention diverted from potential danger as when he watches an attractive stranger while crossing a street. Second, he may disregard a behavioral principle as when he is dishonest without concern for his reputation.

People tend to think of principles as something scientific that is learned from a textbook or from a college course. But principles are ever present in nature, where any person can notice them.

What child ever learned how to balance himself while taking his first few steps by reading a textbook?

Principles determine that action causes reaction, that water expands as it freezes, and that gases can be compressed. Those principles are taught, but significant principles exist that are not taught.

The Basic Law

Principles determine that a person cannot walk through a closed door, that he must breathe both in and out, and that he cannot nourish his body on broken glass—even though no textbook says so.

Anybody can readily see that principles do exert control, and that everybody must act in accord with principles if he is to have a satisfactory life.

Many principles are so very obvious that people automatically take them into account without giving them conscious attention. Everybody sees that they must be obeyed. A person who failed to live in accord with them, along with a multitude of principles which are less obvious, would clearly experience one trouble after another. The reason is that genuine principles are natural laws.

They are self-enforcing. No person can outwit them however he tries. Anyone who could outwit them would be able to walk right through closed doors, violate rules of breathing, and thrive on broken glass—in outright defiance of reality.

Principles are obviously pieces of reality that both determine and explain how things work.

Nothing ever happens in a person's daily affairs that is not controlled by principles. Consequently anybody who understands principles should understand what causes trouble. That enables him to avoid the trouble that arises because principles are disregarded.

It should be easy to realize that people get into trouble by disregarding principles necessary to safe living. However, those principles are often disregarded—with dangerous and sometimes disastrous results.

Principles determine that nobody is healthy if he regularly gets insufficient sleep, that a person who keeps antagonizing others has arguments, and that everybody needs to learn and notice what he is doing as the way to prevent accidents and stay out of trouble.

Those principles are commonly understood, but they are also commonly disregarded. That naturally leads to trouble. Some factor causes people to disregard them, and that factor is given attention next.

Counterfeit Principles

NO SANE person steps off the edge of a high roof expecting to glide gently downward by power of will. He may urgently desire the applause that such a spectacular accomplishment might engender, but he is unable to make either of the two common mistakes by which people invite their trouble.

In the above situation, he cannot divert his attention from the potential danger. Nor can he successfully disregard the obvious principle of gravity. But every person is inclined to make those mistakes on many occasions when danger or an applicable principle is less easily recognized.

Principles are derived from natural laws, and they all operate together to produce a resultant force that is completely dependable. Consider, for example, the way a person rides a bicycle. Whenever he leans for a turn, he must instinctively and precisely adjust to the influences of gravity and centrifugal force.

If he fails to do that, he loses his balance. If he succeeds, he keeps his balance. In either case the effect is precisely determined by the cause.

It is a genuine principle that a person loses his balance unless he properly adjusts to influences from all natural laws. That implies another genuine principle: ***A person can depend on natural laws to make himself safe in every situation that arises.***

Any person should easily see that depending on natural laws in the form of genuine principles can make him safe in physical situations. But the clear implication is that depending on natural laws also makes a person safe in every other situation.

For example, in his dealings with people.

Experimenters have shown that disregard for the principles of natural law is what engenders people's quarrels, bickerings, misunderstandings, disagreements and outright battles. The person who carefully analyzes the details sees how. But perhaps the details are most easily described in relation to matters that involve formation of compulsions.

Consider a person starting a compulsion to engage in smoking, drinking, drug abuse or other crime.

He disregards approaching danger by putting his attention on a wanted result. He also disregards genuine principles of natural law by substituting what in this book is described as counterfeit principles of self-made laws. They obscure his danger.

Irrationality

A YOUNG person sees friends indulging in wrong behavior. He desires acceptance and fears rejection unless he joins them. He suspects his failure to do so may be held against him, and his suspicion is strengthened when they chide him and call him chicken. Quickly he joins them.

The wrong behavior suggests a dire consequence: for example, possible death from lung cancer or cirrhosis of the liver in the cases of smoking or drinking. But the young friend has no intention of persisting long enough to form a compulsion. Nor does he expect to invite a dire consequence; he just wants to be in with the crowd. So he disregards genuine principles telling him how abuse of his body causes present trouble and more problems in the future.

Quite possibly he was told not to take part in the proposed activity by his parents, school authorities and even by law. However, anyone can break or outwit man-made laws so he decides no real obstacle stands in the way of his freedom to act as he pleases.

Because of his motives and proddings by his friends, self-made laws start popping into his mind: "I can do as I please if I don't get caught." "Unless I go along with the crowd, I won't be accepted." "I don't have to keep it up, so I'll pretend I like it." "Everybody does it, so it must be all right."

In his mind natural laws and man-made laws are pushed aside and self-made laws start the action that points toward formation of a compulsion. Whenever necessary, more self-made laws are formed and stored in memory for future use however they apply.

The persons who took part in the research leading to these findings testify that this pattern approximates the procedure by which their compulsive wrong behavior started and gained control.

Three distinct steps are often involved. ***First, natural laws are disregarded. Second, man-made laws are ignored. Third, self-made laws are formulated and adopted.*** Each of the self-made laws became what is described as a counterfeit principle because it lacks proper conformity with nature.

Thus another genuine principle is made evident: Trouble is invited by substitution of counterfeit principles for genuine principles. Obviously that principle also constitutes a natural law of behavior.

The fact that self-made laws are unnatural should now be evident. They are not a part of creation and consequently are not enforced by nature. They must be enforced by the person himself. Enforcing them is difficult and frequently impossible because they tend to disregard both man-made and natural laws.

Often they actually contradict those laws.

The analysis of self-made laws quickly shows that they are not rational. They always contain details that contradict man-made or natural laws and consequently lead to trouble. They frequently contradict other self-made laws he formed and adopted and frequently cause him to oppose other persons who have adopted self-made laws of their own.

Consider the start of a compulsion to smoke as it might be initiated in the mind of a young person.

He has read the warnings in cigarette advertising. He has been told not to smoke and has seen kids punished for smoking. He has heard storekeepers refuse to sell cigarettes to kids because it is illegal. And he has been told that smoking cuts down wind, involves risk of fire, and invites emphysema, heart trouble and lung cancer.

He has thus been subjected to the influences of both man-made and natural laws. Despite that, he starts forming self-made laws that contradict what he has learned. And the self-made laws win.

Genuine Principles

THE REASON the self-made laws win is that they flow out of a person's intent to get his own way. That intent is what makes him a slave to his urges against his own best interests. It forces him to make choices in accord with his likes and dislikes—not because of likes and dislikes but because that is how he determines what is his own way.

Trying to get his own way is the only system he knows. He always lived under it. He equates it with freedom although it enslaves him to the trouble his urges so frequently lead him into.

At first he cannot escape from that system.

He cannot directly change his likes and dislikes because of his intent. He cannot change his intent because his attention is diverted from it by likes and dislikes. But when he understands clearly and correctly what is involved, he can put attention on his intent, take it away from his likes and dislikes, and put it on reality. After he has done that, his likes and dislikes begin rearranging themselves in accord with reality rather than with his urges.

That change takes him out of the relative system of reasoning in which decisions are based on urges. It introduces him to the absolute system of reasoning in which decisions are based on reality.

The same driving force continues to propel him, but it sends him in a different direction. Instead of controlling him in accord with urges based on his motives, it controls him in accord with the reality he formerly did not notice because of his urges.

That provides him with a new plan of life.

Instead of subjecting him to control by urges causing trouble and frustration, it brings him safety and success. Looking back, he sees that what he had regarded as freedom was really a misleading substitute. As new horizons open before him, he feels a new kind of exhilaration and excitement that he had never previously experienced.

He discovers a whole new world of wonders.

With growing pleasure he discovers that there is a clear distinction between the counterfeit principles by which people get into trouble and the genuine principles that enable people to become safe.

Rationality

PEOPLE DO not easily realize that their lives are almost entirely based on compulsions. They are born with the intent to get their own way. Consequently they let their likes and dislikes be dictated by that intent and do their best to live in accord with the resulting pattern of urges.

They feel a compulsion to act on those urges.

What they regard as freedom of choice is merely the freedom to continue in slavery to their urges. The result is a compulsive kind of life that misleads people by masquerading as real freedom.

Each person does have a genuine freedom: the freedom to change intent from wrong to right.

Everybody who fully understands the foregoing information regards the intent to act on urges as irrational and wrong. He regards the intent to act on reality as rational and right. His understanding causes him to reverse his basic approach to life.

Before that reversal, he accepts dictation from his urges. He lets them enslave him by controlling his wants. It is as if a subtle, insidious force had reached into his head and turned a mental switch the wrong direction, sending him into a life of willing servitude during which he disregards numerous pieces of reality so he can get his own way.

That attitude contradicts his real interests.

The disregarded pieces of reality are still there, and they cause trouble for him. Because he disregarded those pieces of reality, he does not realize how he invited the trouble. Consequently he persists in his destructive program of life without any awareness of the mechanism behind it—without the awareness that there is a means of remedy.

That goes on until he understands what is happening.

Then, in effect, he turns the switch the other way. He does it by deciding that he will no longer accept dictation from his urges and that he will turn to reality for his future decisions.

That change leads to a life of rationality.

At first a person is afraid to make the change. All his life he has been living by urges. He trusts them. They point him in the direction of what he expects sooner or later will bring him happiness and real satisfaction.

Those expectations are never realized.

The reason is that urges cause a person to disregard the pieces of reality that must be taken into account to cause happiness and satisfaction. They are the same pieces of reality that he dislikes, because he is afraid of them. So he refuses to consider them, although if he did, he would discover that his fear is entirely groundless.

He is afraid to consider the possibility that he does indeed cause his own trouble, but until he considers the reality, he cannot make that discovery.

Consequently he cannot stop his trouble.

He is afraid he will not get his own way. But he is not getting it. He is afraid he will have to take action he dislikes. But he is already taking it. He is afraid he will be unable to do what he likes. But he is already unable. He is afraid he will lose his friends. But that fear is part of what locks him in trouble. He is afraid of becoming irrational. But fear is already making him irrational because it diverts his attention away from reality.

Irrationality is the result of disregarding reality. The way to achieve rationality is to look directly at the precise reality of whatever is happening and take right action.

Life Without Fear

REALITY APPEARS harsh to many persons because they misunderstand it. Looking at reality is as easy as noticing an approaching vehicle before crossing a street. It brings protection that makes a person safe, but people frequently think of reality in ways that tend to give it a bad reputation.

In trying situations, they have been told to face reality. Therefore, reality tends to be associated in their minds with numerous trying situations.

What could be more trying than awakening in a hospital and discovering that you are there because you failed to notice the reality of an approaching vehicle? Noticing the reality might obviously have prevented the trying situation. That example shows how a person avoids trouble by looking at reality.

The hospitalized victim of an automobile accident might easily remember that he did indeed fail to look for the approaching vehicle. But many causes of trouble are more difficult to identify.

After a person gets the trouble he invited by disregarding reality, he usually fails to realize that he invited it because the sequence of cause and effect is almost always more obscure. Also he is so busy struggling with the resulting situation of harsh reality that he rarely looks for the earlier reality he disregarded. That reality is the kind he thinks of when he judges that reality is harsh.

He may think of the problems he cannot solve: misbehavior by his children, arguments with his spouse, dissatisfaction with his employment, his stomach ulcer, difficulty meeting credit card payments and perhaps a multitude of other problems.

He tries to forget his difficulties by reading books and

newspapers or watching TV, going to movies or nightclubs, submerging himself in some work or hobby, getting drunk or high on drugs. He engages in various activities to escape from the reality that is indeed harsh.

An understanding person knows that disregarding reality invites trouble. He also knows that there is a successful formula for escape.

There is indeed, and it is being used by enough persons to demonstrate that it is liberating.

Ignored reality causes trouble. Learning to inspect that reality prevents the trouble. It also eliminates the need to deal with recurring trouble. It constitutes a formula for escaping into the life without fear.

Unscientific Thinking

INSTEAD OF avoiding harsh reality, a person should put his mind on it. That statement may cause people to cringe but only because they are using the wrong, relative system of reasoning.

Changing to the absolute system is releasing.

Considering harsh reality provides a powerful incentive for change. But something more is needed than improvement in watching for approaching vehicles or even anticipating possible death from lung cancer after forty years of smoking. Nobody could develop enough ingenuity and caution to anticipate the outcome of every potentially dangerous situation. Instead, a person should put attention on causes as they arise, something he cannot do while he keeps attention on results.

That is the danger of relative system thinking.

Reasoning from an urge directs attention toward a wanted

The Basic Law

result and away from danger. The urge suggests that the end justifies the means, and that drives attention toward forming counterfeit principles intended to produce wanted results.

People's urges spontaneously cause emotion.

What is here called an urge does not arise from natural laws nor from man-made laws. Instead, urges arise from self-made laws, resulting from personal motives that tend to disregard reality. Consequently urges invite frustration and when the frustration comes, the emotion is intensified.

By remembering situations of that kind, a person is able to reason from their reality. By doing so, he sees evidence that under emotion intelligence is reduced. While his attention is directed toward a wanted result, it is diverted from the reality that would show the invitation to trouble.

That creates the precise situation in which trouble is often invited without a person's awareness.

The following are additional self-made laws that a person commonly installs in his mind: "I can get away with this if I'm careful." "I have to take advantage of every opportunity that arises." "This is my big chance." "As long as I get what I want, nothing else matters." That is exactly the sort of thinking that produces self-made laws. The resulting counterfeit principles lead to urges that invite all kinds of trouble.

Scientific Thinking

DECISIONS BASED on man-made laws keep a person out of trouble with the authorities. Decisions based on natural or God-made laws keep a person out of trouble with all creation—including authorities. Decisions based on self-made laws move a person toward ultimate disaster because they divert attention away from natural laws.

The foregoing explanation is how man does indeed invite his own trouble. When a person traces out the sequence of cause and effect he sees how that trouble can be ended. The whole story can be read from the reality of whatever happens—something earlier referred to as the book of life.

Some persons have objected to that wording. They say it contradicts scriptural writings, but their comments indicate superficial thinking.

No concept in this book represents the opinion of a person. Instead, every concept was learned by looking directly at the reality from which every other person must also learn. Any scriptural or other writings that contradict pieces of reality would clearly be incorrect.

Reasoning from reality makes a person safe.

There are better scriptural correlations with reality than the religionists have commonly noticed. For one, God is quoted as having said, "I will put my law in their inward parts, and write it in their hearts." What is more clearly lodged in the system of a person's thinking than the law of gravity?

That is where a basic natural law should be.

People have polluted the sanctuary of their hearts and minds with self-made laws. During moments of emotion, people form them in profusion. They turn out to be what is warring against the natural laws.

Every self-made law is a separate and distinct counterfeit principle that gets used as a premise in a person's routine processes of thinking. Consequently those wrong premises become the bases of decisions that are misleading because they are not based on genuine principles.

Clearly seen, the sequence of cause and effect looks simple. However, it is dangerous because counterfeit principles lead to counterfeit conclusions and are unconsciously used as premises.

The Basic Law

A person seldom recognizes his processes of logic while they are in operation. Consider an example: Oncoming vehicles endanger people in their path; I am in such a path; I should move. That example makes the point.

It expresses a genuine principle. It then expresses what may be a fact from which a safe conclusion clearly follows. It represents sound reasoning.

People use genuine principles in various routine decisions. So they lift their feet to step up, talk loudly enough to make themselves heard, and avoid throwing lighted matches into wastebaskets. People also use counterfeit principles in their routine thinking, causing wrong conclusions.

Every counterfeit principle invites trouble.

A person may decide, "I can always get my way by trying." That is a counterfeit principle that cannot be effectuated. The person who continues to reason from it is sure to become frustrated.

No natural law leads a person to adopt self-made laws. Nor does any man-made law. What does?

Only his persistent intent to get his own way.

Because he continues reasoning from counterfeit principles and the urges they engender, he keeps traveling a wrong path of life—until he understands his mistakes.

Then he sees that no action is right unless it conforms with natural laws and genuine principles. He sees that self-made laws make a person inattentive to nature's basic law of behavior: Right action gets right results, whereas wrong action gets wrong results.

Intelligence

IN CONSIDERING the foregoing information, a newcomer to it necessarily uses the relative system of reasoning. Consequently he may dislike the information because it tells him that he should abandon all his urges and inclinations that are based on the motives he is incessantly trying to satisfy.

At first the change makes no sense to him.

Rarely does anyone attempt a careful analysis of the information. Instead, people may turn away from it because that is just what their urges and inclinations make them want to do. If pressed into considering the information, they may react by forming judgments about it. Instantly the judgments become counterfeit principles that insulate their minds.

That has happened even to scientific thinkers.

It is a purpose of scientific thinking to exclude personal opinions and to include every pertinent perception of reality. After a person has done both, he knows that his conclusions are correct.

He sees that real intelligence is an impersonal quality that is expressed when a person reasons from reality.

He sees that there is a misleading kind of intelligence in the relative system of reasoning that depends on urges arising from motives. He also sees that there is a natural intelligence in the absolute system that transcends any kind of meddling.

He learns to depend on that intelligence.

By depending on it, he discovers the principle of principles: Counterfeit principles are misleading; therefore, only genuine principles should be used as premises on which decisions are based.

He learns to eliminate counterfeit principles.

As soon as he tries, he can learn to recognize them. He can also learn to find the genuine principles in the reality of his life. After he gets the idea, dropping counterfeit principles becomes a fascinating pursuit until he succeeds in reasoning only in the absolute system of genuine principles based on reality.

The Basic Law

AT THE heart of people's objections, there is a moral consideration. It relates to the distinctions between right and wrong that cannot be determined solely by reference to man-made or self-made laws but can be determined with the assistance of natural or God-made laws found in reality.

People are slow to accept moral considerations.

They have an unfortunate inclination to imagine that right action sometimes gets wrong results and that wrong action sometimes gets right results.

They use that thinking to justify their errors.

People who have learned to reason from reality understand what is involved. *They support each other in right action while withholding support for wrong action. They observe that the basic law of absolute right is the natural law governing human behavior. They rely on it as naturally as they rely on gravity. They live by its principle: Always think, say and do what is right.*

They enjoy a genuinely satisfactory plan of life.

Preface to Part III

THIS SECTION describes and explains the basic plan for introducing sanity into the stream of human affairs. Anybody who considers the details carefully enough soon realizes that the plan is entirely natural. It is as natural as gravity, as time, as rotation of the earth and all other reality.

The plan is not invented. It was observed.

Numerous persons were taught to observe it—persons of many ages and both sexes from many walks of life. Once observed, as was stated earlier, it changes a person's approach to the future.

A simple factor often kept it from being observed.

People do not like to consider whatever they regard as anathematic, and they won't consider it. Anathema is misplaced when directed toward the plan that is being discussed here.

Objection to the plan for introducing sanity into the stream of human affairs says something about how confused people's minds have become. It shows that objectors have not yet observed the reality.

Part III

The Basic Plan

PEOPLE LIKE fun, enjoyment, comfort, and a sense of well-being. They like thrills, excitement, feelings of importance. They like having their own way. But they get too little of what they like and too much of what they dislike, so they seek balms.

They go to parties and nightclubs, watch TV, drink, use palliatives and mind-benders and uppers and downers and engage in risky activities.

People submit to a lot of what they dislike.

They dislike being criticized, blamed and condemned. They dislike drudgery, getting teeth drilled by a dentist or undergoing a dangerous operation. Yet they submit to such hardships, sometimes at great cost in money and suffering. They accept hardships whenever they feel the cost of not accepting them is greater than the cost of accepting them.

People have unanswered questions about life.

What could possibly be rational about likes that lead to trouble? Or about dislikes that force a person to reject doing what is rational?

Those particular questions have an answer.

People are driven by urges to act in accord with likes and dislikes that are based on their motives, often unconscious. They keep trying to get what they like and avoid what they dislike. In the process they hurt themselves mentally, emotionally and physically—so they need more and more balm.

Evidence shows that people are living by an irrational

plan of life: acting on urges and getting wrong results. Ordinary corrective measures accomplish little more than to let people continue in the same dreary pattern of problems and trouble. But there is an absolutely rational alternative: ***acting on reality and getting right results.***

Persons who are doing it all say that it works.

Escape from Trouble

ACTING ON urges predestines people to form compulsions they cannot stop. The reason is that they willingly accept the dictates of their urges without realizing that they are inviting trouble.

Urges are supported only by human authority.

Acting on impulses from reality is safe because reality is a part of creation. Rather than being based on human authority, reality is based on the natural authority that utterly controls whatever exists and however it operates.

Reality has the true authority of the Creator.

When understood, there is a basic plan of control that replaces a person's urges with an intent to reason from reality.

TWO PLANS of life are available: one based on people's urges and the other based on reality. Conventionally people live by the plan based on their urges although they dislike many of its consequences. At first they may dislike the plan based on reality because they feel it might force them into an unattractive way of life.

Some incautiously shut their minds to it, continue acting on urges and go on living by hope. If so, hope is about all they ever get because their hope stays unfulfilled. If they surmount their dislike, they begin to enjoy a better life.

The Basic Plan

The plan based on reality does seem shocking at first. To some it seems too idealistic. It consternates conventional people, and they hesitate to consider it. They tend to condemn it before they understand it. That is irrational. When they understand it, they realize that the plan based on reality is scientific, religious and essential to the elimination of problems and trouble that beset people so long as their urges control their decisions.

People keep struggling to fulfill their dreams by seeking fame, wealth and high position. They often attempt to dominate other people and force changes in their behavior. No matter what success they seem to achieve, they want more.

That pattern repeatedly appears in the public press.

Television newscasts report regularly on the frequency with which lives of the rich and famous end in disappointment and despair. Often they describe the tragic lives of persons blessed with prosperous careers who are so desperate they resort to alcohol and other drugs, popular treatments and even suicide.

Those tragic consequences result from allowing urges to dictate a person's plan of life. They do not result from living by reality's plan of life. On the contrary, careful attention to the appropriate reality promptly lifts a person out of the desperate consequences of his frustrated hopes. There are people proving it.

They understand the basic plan of control which enabled them to end their dislike of what at first seemed unattractive. They want more people to know that the basic plan naturally improves the thinking and behavior of anyone who is given information about it and studies it until he understands it.

They see the basic plan as the natural method for getting the whole human race out of trouble. They see it as the master plan for a life of true satisfaction.

The persons who understand see a formula at work. It is as simple as the formula that makes a person wait so he will be safe before crossing the street. It is as simple as the formula that makes a person give instinctive respect to gravity so he won't be hurt.

They know that everybody who understands the formula advances to a far better way of life.

Suppositional Reasoning

THE USE of suppositional reasoning is helpful because it enables a person to advance from known reality to probabilities that might prove to constitute reality if carefully tested for verification and consequent adoption. Anybody who tests the results of suppositional reasoning as recorded here is going to get many remarkable surprises.

Begin by considering the existing reality.

The existing reality is that a person keeps trying to get his or her own way, that he or she attempts to satisfy urges, and that in doing so each one frequently disregards reality. It becomes clear that some plan of control is needed to replace urges with the intent to reason from reality before rationality can be introduced into the stream of human affairs.

Suppositional reasoning does not require that a person believe what is said as preparation for understanding. Obviously there is no need for beliefs in the pattern of thinking that is based on reality.

Contacting reality produces knowledge.

One basic tool of suppositional reasoning is the implication. If viewed with proper precautions, an implication may be used to disclose valid information that is not otherwise available.

The Basic Plan

A person may be so eager to cross a street that he resents a warning from a stranger who shouts, "Stop!" He may form the false implication that he is being controlled and disregard the correct implication that would make him safe.

One form of reality is natural law. Natural law is an inarguable fact. Who argues against gravity? It simply exists. As a part of creation, it is not subject to human whims. Nobody owns it, and nobody can alter it no matter how hard he may try. Natural law in any other form is just as coercive as gravity, the instant its reality is noticed.

That introduces the topic of coercive logic.

Many persons consider that term frightening. They think it warns of forced compliance. They call it irreligious and unscientific. Actually it is merely a description of the way reality works.

Does anything sensibly contradict reality?

Religion deals with reality's origin. Science deals with its results. A religionist who understands coercive logic calls it religious. A scientist who understands it calls it scientific. True coercive logic is a matter of reality, not belief. The techniques of coercive logic differ from conventional scientific method. Religionists and scientists should not ignore behavioral reality—where both can meet.

It is a principle of scientific method that findings are presented in a way that permits duplication by other qualified persons. That is also true of coercive logic. It provides a reliable methodology convincing to everybody who follows its logic. Bad reactions result from people's judging it to be disagreeable before they understand it.

If they consider the information carefully enough, they become aware that there is a simple and direct formula for determining what is false and what is true in the field of behavior.

The formula is so fundamental that it actually sets a person free from the need to depend on truth as a basis of reasoning. *The formula is not to look from information to how it may satisfy urges, but to look from information to how it correlates with reality.*

The Danger of Believing

PEOPLE TEND to accept information they like and reject information they dislike. They do that more or less with little regard for its correctness—an unsound basis of reasoning.

It is commonly thought that a person should believe what is true and reject what is false. But even that may lead into a subtle kind of pitfall. People need coercive logic because of a deceptive quality about truth that enables truth itself to mislead.

If believed, truth provides an unsound basis of reasoning because truth must then be accepted on faith—in which case no attention is given reality.

When truth is unknown and is needed, people are tempted to seek a substitute. But neither truth nor its substitute is coercive in the sense that reality is coercive. Obviously the blind acceptance of supposed truth on someone's word that it is truth opens a person to unreliable influence.

Who decides what is truth or untruth?

People offer each other supposed truth in the form of testimony—both in court and elsewhere. The testimony may come from an expert or a layman. It may come from anybody, even a child. It may be true or untrue. In either case it is still just testimony until it is buttressed by proof. The fact is that people seriously misunderstand proof. Additional testimony does not constitute proof except in the legal sense. It is not genuine proof.

There is only one genuine proof: reality.

The Basic Plan

Every discerning person should be able to see that successful use of testimony as a tool of persuasion enables people to mislead one another.

Ordinarily people have powerful incentives to mislead because they want to gain and keep advantages and to avoid and evade disadvantages. But no person is misled by reasoning from reality.

Of course, everybody is misled by others in the normal activity of life, and it makes people cautious. Consequently people often refuse to consider another person's version of supposed truth. The resulting situation is so confusing that people assume that they may as well be guided by likes and dislikes and urges and compulsions—which they usually want to keep in order to get the balm.

That helps people maintain the fiction that they should keep on trying to get their own way.

What Constitutes Proof

IN SOME areas of life, a person is virtually infallible. He finds his way home, recognizes close friends and relatives in public places, and remembers his own name. That is because people usually are well aware of those details of reality.

In other areas people get confused. They often forget to do important work, disregard the welfare of others and arrive late for appointments. That is because they fail to stay in touch with reality. But whenever they are confused, direct awareness of the appropriate reality ends that part of the confusion.

If someone tells you that a mutual friend is dead, you certainly do not go on believing he is dead after you see him walking down the street. If you learn you are waiting on the wrong corner for a bus, you certainly do not go on waiting there after you see the bus stop at another corner.

Recognition of reality changes people's minds.

Obviously a person does not persist in believing an untruth after he knows the truth. He does not learn the truth by being told it; in that case, he can only balance one statement against the other and then decide which to believe—if either. Even if he changes his mind, he has only a statement to support his new belief, and he cannot actually know whether that statement is correct until he checks the reality.

The foregoing comments direct attention to the reality that nobody really knows the truth when all he has is information from another person. That is enough to show the risk of reasoning from truth. It shows what is meant by saying nobody is expected to believe what is said here. It also shows how looking at reality makes a person independent of human authority. It shows exactly why he should look to reality for true understanding of human behavior.

Ordinarily people can depend on what is said by experts in the fields of mathematics, chemistry and engineering; but in the field of human behavior, people often depend on false information in a belief that it is correct. Because there is so much trouble in a person's affairs, he cannot reasonably hope to resolve it by reasoning merely from information.

He needs to reason from the reality it describes.

Reasoning from reality quite often contradicts a person's urges. Allowing urges to control a decision keeps attention off reality, and in that case, information may be misunderstood. *When it is a person's intent to look at reality, he does. When he sees it, he is made independent of the information. What is more significant, he also becomes independent of the person who gives him the information.*

He becomes able to reason from the reality.

It comes as a surprise to most persons that, literally speaking, nobody is really dependent on a supposed statement of truth. If he believes it, he is depending on the person who makes the statement. Usually it also comes as a surprise that a person does not see the reality while he is depending on the person who makes the statement of truth.

If a person tries to reason from truth, he is in danger of reasoning from untruth. He cannot know whether it is truth or untruth until he checks the reality. Then he reasons not from truth nor untruth but from reality. That is what makes him safe.

From this it is obvious that both truth and untruth require reality to provide safety. Contacting the appropriate reality is needed to establish the proof. Its validity is independent of every person.

Reality puts an end to any urge it contradicts.

The Logic of Reality

MOST PERSUASION arises because of urges based on people's conscious and unconscious motives to compete, show authority, prove intelligence, establish supremacy and gain advantages in a variety of other ways.

Such persuasion requires use of personal force.

Personal force has only artificial authority, whereas real authority is the force of coercive logic and is never the logic of a person. It is the logic of reality. The best a person can do is to direct attention to the reality—and let it do the work. That is enough to show the fault of ordinary persuasion.

The force of coercive logic is illustrated by what is commonly known as the self-evident fact.

Strictly speaking, no fact can be self-evident. It is only a concept described in a sentence or held in the mind. It becomes what is known as self-evident when the reality that it describes is observed.

The reality is what is coercive. Not the fact.

If a person tells you he is alive, you can see the evidence for yourself. But if you hear a voice saying the same words, you could be hearing a recording of a person long deceased. Only reference to the correct reality makes a fact self-evident.

In addition, a fact properly described as self-evident, cannot be proved. A person who demands proof shows he is willing to deny the proof that is already evident. He also shows he is not reasoning from reality but from his own urges.

If you tell someone that you are alive and he demands proof, nothing is to be gained by providing it. He has already denied the proof he was shown and that any honest person would have accepted.

Some people confuse themselves and others by saying no one can prove his own existence. Perhaps not. But no honest person demands proof after he is confronted with obvious reality. Even in a court, where proof is considered vital, a person is not required to prove his existence.

A person who denies a self-evident fact proves that he is simply trying to get his own way.

This introduces a spectacularly important kind of information that experts in human behavior apparently have not observed. When understood, application of that information renders behavioral research so simple that it makes the cause of human trouble instantly obvious. Rather than requiring the facilities of a psychological laboratory, a young child is able to make reliable observations.

His understanding is dependable enough that he can solve problems and prevent troubles so common to children they are thought to be unavoidable.

Telescopes, microscopes and other instruments are needed to bring many details of reality within the scope of a person's observation. Without them, he cannot notice molecules of water, for example, or observe the reality that each molecule contains two atoms of hydrogen combined with one atom of oxygen. But ordinary people have access to the facts that explain the true cause of erratic human behavior.

A person is not confused by the unavailability of information but from the fact that he and others evade the reality that would give them the information. That is true of laymen and experts alike. If people totally stopped evading reality, they could become behavioral experts. They could make observations that would provide definitive information about human behavior even though they could not make similar observations about the behavior of atoms.

Accessibility of Information

THE PROCEDURE is so simple and obvious that each person who is given it tends to experience a disruptive emotional reaction. One kind of person denies the correctness of the information. Another kind announces that he already understands it. Still another kind makes both those mistakes.

The reasons are very largely unconscious.

People are driven by urges which force them to keep trying for all the advantages they can get.

A person's urges drive him to establish supremacy in as many ways as he can. That forces people to compete. For unconscious reasons that they fail to notice, people tend to compete with everybody who seems to threaten their efforts to be supreme.

Even those efforts are largely unconscious.

People are so busy competing that they do not put their minds on the reality that would provide the information needed to expose and correct false implications caused by thinking based on urges.

Instead of seeking reality, people seek improved status. When they get information they think may provide it, reality is ignored in favor of their urges. They accept the information they like, utilizing it however they please with little regard for reality. Simultaneously they try to discredit the source of the information so that the person providing it will be unable to compete with them in using it.

That has been an almost universal reaction to the information presented in this section. Of course, people tend to deny it. Their denial is not willful but is dictated by urges and results from evasion of the reality that would give them safe knowledge.

If people understood the consequence of their evasion, they would try to stop it at once. That is demonstrated by the persons who do understand it and did immediately make that change. People cannot get out of trouble until they stop evading reality. To do that, they have to decide to become honest, something that the experimenters have proved can be done.

The influential people have been slowest about changing, and that is understandable because they naturally assume they have much to protect. But a person abandons that notion when he realizes what is at stake, and he joins others who are setting the new pattern.

Adoption of Honesty

SURELY THERE are perceptive persons who are willing to admit that the information is correct without wanting to

The Basic Plan

steal it or discredit its source. Surely there are persons who can admit that they made those mistakes in their past reactions.

They are the persons who can become honest.

A person who refuses to admit his dishonesty is still dishonest. Honest people reserve their highest regard for those persons who decide to adopt absolute honesty as their motivating factor, because it is essential to absolute right.

They know that absolute honesty is not an inborn trait and that it must be developed. They know that absolute honesty is impossible for a person who reasons from urges because of the contradictory nature of urges. They know that anybody who persistently compares his thinking and conversation with reality will see that in the past he has been appallingly unfactual.

He will recognize that he has concealed and misrepresented his motives, has projected images that have falsified him to others, and has created many fantasies he used to help him escape from reality.

He will see that he has not understood honesty.

He will discover that he has actually tried to do and say what would help him to make a good impression on others and best enable him to satisfy his urges. He will recognize that any apparent honesty he happened to express was just a tool he used in the constant attempt to get his own way.

He will see that such honesty is not absolutely honest.

He will also recognize that departures from honesty have a confusing effect on him by separating his mind from reality. He will make a decision to drop urges as a basis of reasoning and adopt reality in their place. He will want everybody else to make the same change because he will know that making the change is the only route to true rationality.

He will not be ashamed of his past dishonesty.

The reason is that everybody who understands what has

been happening realizes that the great proportion of all dishonesty is an impersonal kind of dishonesty forced on people by the relative system of reasoning into which each person is born.

Because people reason from urges under that system, they are compulsively dishonest in a huge number of ways without being able to recognize that fact—until they understand how to reason from natural principles in the absolute system of reasoning. Then they change their plan of life. They escape from the relative system by adopting the absolute system of reasoning and taking the action called for by the reality. They base decisions on the intent to think, say and do what is right.

Enough people have made that change to prove that it gets precisely the results predicted by the theoretical reasoning that everybody would accept without hesitation if people were not blocked by urges that compel them to evade reality.

Every person can escape from the wrong plan of life by adopting reality as his exclusive basis of reasoning. Reasoning from reality has the effect of forcing the dishonesty out of his thinking processes. Every person who understands the basic plan of nature wants to make that change, and in due course, he does.

He knows it is a reliable plan of life.

He knows that what is right flows out of reality, that it always contradicts whatever is wrong, that it always works, and that it is correctly defined as whatever the situation calls for.

That is why he adopts the intent to have right intent as his way of life and accepts his natural plan.

Obvious Evidence

HE HAS no sense of loss because he sees that reasoning from urges has kept him in trouble and that reasoning from reality allows him to escape.

That opens his mind to obvious evidence.

He realizes that many of the modern scientific developments were made necessary only by people's irrationality: for example, the atom bomb. He sees that there is a simple way for people to get along with one another without fighting, a way that does not depend on abstruse reasoning beyond the grasp of the average adult or child.

Nobody needs a scientific instrument to see examples of human behavior. Nor does he need the help of experts to find simple evidence that shows what is wrong about human affairs.

After a person learns to look for it, he sees abundant evidence. Suddenly he wants to share it.

He may make the mistake of taking his new-found information to some expert for evaluation, and he may get some wrong advice.

In past years many experts advised people to reject the information. Their eagerness to turn people away from it showed their fear of it. Why? Perhaps because they were controlling people by telling them to believe supposed truth and realized they would lose that control if people reasoned from reality.

Those experts did not understand the force of reality.

A person who understands control by reality does not yield to the force of misguided persuasion. Rather, he yields to the coercive logic of reality for the same reason as he yields to gravity. And because he understands the force of reality, nobody can persuade him that he should not live by it.

A person starts life without that understanding. In its place he has what might be described as the urge to act on his urges even when those urges keep getting him in trouble. He has other urges to stay out of trouble, and that confronts him with a contradiction to reconcile—and strong incentive to do it.

To the extent that he knows how wrong action causes trouble, he develops the intent to take right action. But at first he has gaps in his understanding.

When he learns that reasoning from urges causes his trouble, his urge to prevent trouble makes him consider reality. At first reality seems harsh. That is because of the reality he invited by disregarding reality: for example, the time he got fired because he disregarded the risk of doing slipshod work.

With complete understanding, his intent to stop his trouble by looking at reality supplants his urge to disregard it. Then he sees that reality offers a message: Avoid harsh reality by paying attention to the benign reality that prevents trouble. He notices examples when he looks for them.

Soon he becomes able to remember many examples that show the nature of reality. As he concentrates on taking right action, he sees the evidence that changes his life.

By looking beneath the surface of that evidence, he also sees the nature of the basic plan.

It is a plan that has the effect of inducing him to drop his plan of life. He abandons the idea of reasoning from urges to get his own way, and he adopts the plan of reasoning from reality for all his decisions. Then he starts really getting his way because his way has become the way of reality.

The Astonishing Release

THE BASIC plan is a plan of control that causes a person to abandon his self-conceived plan of life and adopt the natural plan for control of his affairs.

It is a change he makes as soon as he understands.

The basic plan of control can be described as an expression of reality that many persons agree reveals the Creator's basic plan for changing human behavior. Years ago that statement frightened some people. It is not frightening to a person who calmly inspects the facts that are made evident by reality to anybody who honestly looks at it.

Absolute honesty is the key to understanding.

It must be obvious that people who consider this information with the intent to adopt it selfishly while denying its source are people who lack absolute honesty. That defeats them in any effort they may make to increase their authority by using information that depends on absolute honesty.

Everybody needs to know that the authority is in reality.

People avidly search for techniques that promise authority. They should search for techniques that solve their problems. In that search they should remember that nothing has truly solved them; then put their attention on reality.

That illustrates the real nature of right intent.

Some persons have enlarged their understanding by considering some suppositional reasoning that may be actual truth. Reality does not fully confirm it, although those persons say the reasoning does correlate with other recognized reality.

They have put the information to good use.

They have gained a practical awareness of what might be described as the new reality, although it is not new; it just was not seen. The reason it was not seen is because people have let their attention get diverted from it by their urges.

The newly seen reality is that a very basic contradiction exists between the instinctive urges with which a person is born and the reality of what happens in his life. Obviously some factor arises within him that opposes both creation and Creator. It is something the Creator must have intended if omniscient. The implication is that the contradiction must be a part of the Creator's own explicit plan. What might be the reason for that?

What else but to force man's change of intent?

The change of intent is stimulated by correct awareness of the contradiction. It is a change from dishonest, wrong intent to honest, right intent. That certainly correlates with the widespread teachings of a righteous and beneficent Creator.

Consider the way people act when they fail to get their own way. In that situation people are frustrated and unhappy. In anger they may act as if they think they should get their way by shouting, should have the right to act exactly as they please and should be free to ignore any restrictions on their behavior. Their reactions constantly keep them apart from reality on the topics involved with the result that vital pieces of reality are missing from the premises they use when making their decisions.

Until they recognize the importance of reasoning from reality instead of urges, they do not change. After they recognize it, they want to make that change more than they want to do anything else in their lives.

BECAUSE OF urges, a person creates many unreal desires and keeps trying to effectuate them without success. That explains his unwillingness to accept reality as established by the Creator.

He is confronted with a contradiction that has to be reconciled before he can begin a satisfactory life.

A person who reasons from reality reconciles it.

By reasoning from urges, he keeps causing himself trouble. By reasoning from reality, he stops trouble. When he sees and understands the difference, he promptly makes the reconciliation.

Suppositional reasoning suggests that the divine plan thus intends each person to reform by changing his way of life. Perhaps every person who gains that awareness discovers that the law of absolute right has at last been put into his inward parts and written into his heart—fulfilling the basic plan.

Conclusion

Evidence of Things Not Seen

PEOPLE ARE all in trouble not commonly recognized as trouble because such trouble is considered necessary and natural. It is not necessary and it is not natural. Instead it is the result of wrong thinking and the wrong behavior patterns caused by wrong thinking. In a deeper sense, it is the result of a wrong plan of life.

It is a purpose of this book to deal with such matters. On the whole, pursuit of that purpose was often regarded as an expression of effrontery. In fact it is no such thing. It is the direct expression of an awareness that evokes both awe and humility in everybody who gains correct recognition of its importance.

For those persons, belief is replaced by knowledge. What happens to their faith? Something very few persons were prepared to anticipate.

Faith has two common definitions which differ markedly. One of those definitions holds that faith constitutes a kind of belief that is unsupported by proper evidence. The other holds that faith constitutes fidelity to proper obligations, especially those obligations that relate to the Creator.

Persons who understand humanetics have learned that faithful obedience to the Creator is established by faithful observance of every natural law. They have learned that such faith gets astonishing results that are not believable until they are experienced. The reason is that such faith opens a person's mind to perceptions of reality that supplant beliefs with knowledge.

At times religious persons have objected. Their objections are surprising in view of the scriptural statement that faith is the evidence of things not seen. People who reason from reality have learned that faithfulness to every proper obligation does bring evidence of things not seen—along with astonishing benefits.

That requires a very exacting kind of faith. A specific formula has produced great enlargements of faithfulness for persons who have used it.

Notice the reality of any situation that confronts you. Ask yourself what you *want* to do and then what a person reasoning entirely from reality would do. Be sure that it is right. Then do it. Even if the results seem strange, keep on doing what is right in every situation that arises. Anyone who does that shows exacting faith. Nothing less could be completely right.

Steady application of that formula leads a person down the path toward a series of three reversals. First, he reverses his approach to information called humanetics by seeking understanding instead of rejecting it. Second, he reverses his approach to life by deciding to reason exclusively from reality and accept no interference from his urges or motives. Third, he reverses his approach to the future by adopting the natural plan as it is determined by reality.

Nobody can get the new way of life established until he has made those three reversals. All of the people who brought their behavior under control made them successfully, including the youngest of the kids. After that, their progress was dramatic.

Some people have shuddered over that formula: Always think, say and do what is right. They have stronger reason to shudder over failure to live by it. When they discover that its use prevents enormous amounts of trouble, they change. Theoretically they could make all three reversals at one time, just by deciding to make them.

The person who does becomes one of those people who at last intends to let civilization begin.

ADVENTURES IN HUMANETICS

Introduction to Experiential Material

PEOPLE GET edgy when absolute honesty is mentioned. They should be eager to discuss it. The reason is that everybody's security depends on it.

Here is the startling but correct explanation.

People have a very limited definition of what constitutes dishonesty. They may think of it as stealing. They may think of it as something done by one person against another. That can be dishonesty, but it is an almost insignificant part of what is involved. And it is the least important—like the protruding tip of the proverbial iceberg.

What remains hidden is what is important.

It is hidden because each person keeps trying to get his way as dictated by his urges. That is his personal plan. He follows it as though driven by a compulsion.

By observing what happens when frustration arises, people who understand humanetics clearly see the pattern of action that causes trouble.

They observe that urges tend to disregard reality, which is why people take action risky to themselves and others. It leads to sicknesses, accidents, frustrations, failures, conflicts. These are the penalties of living by the personal plan.

People adjust their thinking for risky action by installing distortions of logic: "I'll get my way if it kills me." "Little white lies don't matter." "If other people do it, I can too." "I won't think about results."

Thus they bridge the gaps of rationality.

There is a natural plan that expresses reality.

People who reason directly from reality have no gaps to be bridged. Consequently they have no reason to be dishonest. They discover that absolute honesty cannot actually be tried by a person who has not escaped from the clutches of his urges. They know why people get edgy when absolute honesty is mentioned. And they understand the basic formula for sanity: Always think, say and do what is right; refuse to think, say and do what is wrong.

Contents

STOPPING FAMILY FIGHTS 75
THE DEVIL MADE ME DO IT 96
RELATIONSHIPS 98
GAMES 124

Stopping Family Fights

I RANK sixth in our family of seven children. Three brothers and two sisters are older and one sister is younger.

As a small child, I had few friends in the neighborhood, so I stayed at home, and my older sisters and brothers became my playmates. Well, I shouldn't call them playmates because we didn't really play. We fought. We fought almost from the time we awakened in the morning until we went to sleep at night.

It is true we played games but not without fighting. That meant the strongest one or, at least, the scrappiest usually got his way. We made sure he had to fight to keep it, so the fighting rarely ceased. It was like warfare. Everyone had to hold his ground and, at the same time, invade someone else's.

In all the games, there was a desired position everybody wanted. As the smallest I rarely got it, but I did get other things like bruises, hurt feelings and frustrations.

There was no one younger I could use to relieve my frustrations except my baby sister, and I knew better than to lay a hand on her. Instead, I ran to Mommy. She rescued me from the big bullies. Sometimes she was tied up and couldn't come to my rescue. During those times, I learned to escape by running like hell. When she did settle a matter, I usually got my way. But it led to more trouble. As soon as she left, the fight would start again. I'd hear, "Baby, baby, stick your head in gravy." That was my weak spot. I hated to be called a baby. I yearned for the day when I'd be big enough to beat them up.

My brothers and sisters resented the fact that Mommy took my part, so they often left me out. Soon the only time I played with them was when she wasn't home. Those were my worst times. I'd run off crying to wait till Mommy got home. As soon as she appeared, I'd purposely turn on the waterworks and run to her screaming about what they had done. She'd open the kitchen drawer and grab the wooden spoon. The contents of the drawer jingled and everyone knew to run for it. By that time my tears would have dried, and I'd excitedly yell, "Get 'em, Mom, get 'em!"

After a while my brothers and sisters just stopped playing with me, and I spent practically all my time in front of the television.

When school started, everybody was gone except one sister and me and the baby. We were forced to be together even though we hated it. She was two years older but the same size, so our fights were disasters. We exchanged black eyes, bruises, sore muscles, hurt feelings, torn clothing and broken toys. I hated her, and we had fistfights over every little thing that went wrong.

When I started kindergarten, I was thrilled to get out of the house and away from the family. I met playmates there, and visiting them became my escape hatch. However, my conflict patterns went with me, and I fought with them just as I fought with my family. I insisted on the desired position and usually got it since I made sure my friends were smaller.

My friends' parents disliked my attitude and limited my time with their children. That drove me back home to my family.

At home I changed my ways so I could play with my brothers and sisters. I convinced them I wouldn't go to Mommy if I didn't get my way. Anyway, it had become different with her. She didn't come to my rescue when I screamed.

Instead of punishing them, she told them to knock it off. That had as much effect as telling a baby to stop crying. I was out for myself and had no allies.

As I grew older, my interests changed along with theirs. We ganged up, and mischief became our main line of action. My next older brother was especially inventive, and I learned a lot from him.

One of the games we played was army. That involved building forts, digging ditches, obtaining supplies and occasionally building fires. To play army, we needed certain equipment we didn't have. That wasn't much of an obstacle though because we took things from our house and from the neighbors' yards and garages. We even picked up food supplies from the local candy store by ordering a large bottle of soda so the clerk would have to go into the back room for it. While he was gone, we stuffed our pockets with candy bars.

During preparations for the game, there wasn't much conflict. We had a common interest and knew we had to cooperate to achieve it. When we were ready, it was every man for himself. Even though it was a game, the conflict was quite serious.

Someone would shout, "Bang! You're dead."

"I am not. You missed me."

"I did not. I was only five feet away."

"I'm wearing my bullet-proof vest. Bang!"

"You dirty rat, I'll fix you." The verbal fight ended and the fistfight began. The kid who was beat up lost the war. That honor was usually mine.

As we grew older, verbal fighting replaced most of the fistfighting. I felt a lot safer because my tongue was as sharp as anyone's. We had plenty of hurt feelings but no sore muscles.

An example of our verbal fighting occurred at the dinner table. First, we asked God to make our meal a pleasant one and thanked Him for our food. Then, as soon as the prayer was over, the fighting began. Smart cracks and insults filled the air. Sometimes objects started flying across the table, landing on the plates and splattering food. What we didn't like, we slipped to the dog under the table.

That was the first part of the meal. The second part was even worse—dessert time. Everyone seemed to have a sweet tooth and wanted the most dessert. It caused so many arguments my father measured each portion. No matter how accurate he tried to be, one portion always seemed bigger. One procedure for claiming a dessert was to stick a finger in the piece we wanted. No one else would touch it after that.

Once when a sister and I were slugging each other over dessert, my father told us to read the plaque over the doorway for ten minutes. The words were "Love One Another." I spent the ten minutes devising a scheme to get back at her.

With seven children, there was a lot of damage done to our house. We blamed it on each other even when we had done it ourselves. One time, my parents noticed writing on the dining room wall. We were all called into the living room for a conference. My father described the situation and asked, "Who did it?"

All he heard was, "I didn't," repeated seven times.

The room fell silent. My father was annoyed and started to apply pressure. "What do you mean? It got there by itself?"

We thought if someone didn't admit the crime, we'd all get a beating. We looked at my younger sister. She resisted and wouldn't confess. After we had been sitting in the living room an hour and a half, my older sister took the blame. Instead of whipping her, my father made her clean the wall. That was supposed to let us know that if we told the truth, we wouldn't be punished, but we were afraid to trust him.

We had felt his belt many times and didn't want to risk it.

It was usually my father who threatened us with punishment, and he could hit hard. My mother threatened us indirectly. She'd say, "Wait till your father gets home." Then he would beat the crap out of us. We learned to put extra padding in the rear.

After a few beatings, I started to catch on. I was asking for punishment by getting caught, so I changed my ways. I made darn sure nobody saw me whenever I did something I knew was wrong. I never told my brothers or sisters what I did, because I knew they'd squeal—they loved to witness a good whacking. I also knew that after the whacking, they'd make fun of me. That seemed like a terrible price to pay for not covering my tracks. I often lied to avoid punishment.

A large part of our conflict resulted from competition. We competed over almost everything. We wanted to be the one who ran the fastest, had the best complexion, dressed the coolest or excelled in some other way. We often used our accomplishments to belittle each other, and my best weapon in such an attack was my report card.

After completing my third year in grammar school, I found my report card beside my sister's. Her grades were better than mine. It made me feel dumb. I tore mine up and decided that next year I'd get straight A's. I had to work but I did get the A's. I made sure everybody saw my report card. I boasted about my grades so my brothers and sisters wouldn't call me a dummy. No one did. Instead, I was called "brain" and "teacher's pet." I was embarrassed and angry and plotted how to get back at them.

When my father forced the kids with bad grades to study, I laid it on heavy. During the two-hour study period, I ran in and out of the kitchen pretending I was having a wonderful time. Every once in a while I'd remind them that if they were like me, they wouldn't have to study so hard. They often beat me up afterward, but I couldn't resist putting them down.

By that time, I was fed up with the entire family and wanted them to get out of my life. Then one day after breakfast, Mother called us into the family room. We gathered around not knowing what would happen next. She made an announcement, "All right, kids, I'm going to teach you humanetics."

Everyone groaned and opposition flared, "Oh, come on. You mean I have to go to school all week and then learn humanetics on the weekend?"

My mother hushed us. She insisted we learn humanetics. We knew what that meant. It wasn't the first time she had tried to push humanetics on us. A year ago she had told us that we were going to learn a body of knowledge that would help us solve our problems. We weren't interested. We had been lectured in school, in church and at home by persons who all claimed they were trying to help us solve our problems. Well, we hated it. We'd found their advice had only caused more problems. If humanetics was anything like that, we didn't want anything to do with it. When she brought up the subject again, we put up a fight. No one was going to tell us how to solve our problems. So after enough opposition, she gave up. I was glad. The family went about its normal way of life: one fight after another.

As time passed, we drifted further apart. My brothers and sisters were all doing their own thing. I was jealous because I seemed to be doing the same thing year after year—nothing.

Then my older brothers and sisters got involved in new and exciting things such as smoking, drinking, drugs, and sex. I thought it would be exciting to follow the same path. They seemed to enjoy what they were doing, especially my next older brother. He was involved in the cool life. I admired him and thought he was brave for taking so many risks. I knew drugs and drinking were risky. You could take an overdose of drugs or get drunk, and your parents or the cops might find out. My admiration of him caused me to want to be like him. I shut off my criticisms and tried to be nice to him.

Sometimes it worked and sometimes it didn't. I decided to let him get away with only so much. When he passed the limit, I did something about it. That worked pretty well, but it wasn't easy. I had to exert self-control to suppress my emotional blowups and often relieved myself by picking on my little sister.

My relationship with him appeared to improve while my relationship with my little sister went from bad to worse. Even though I was nice to him, he wasn't nice to me. In fact, he was mean. But I would cover up my hatred by laughing at his insults. While I laughed, I often fantasized about some clever plot I might fiendishly execute to put him at my mercy.

I thought he would be nicer to me if I copied him. He had long hair, cool clothes, and a dirty way of talking, so I changed my ways to match his. I pressured my mother for jeans and flannel shirts and let my hair grow. I learned the definitions of the popular four-letter words. I was determined to impress him with my new, cool style. He wasn't impressed and, as a matter of fact, became more insulting.

"Look at Mr. Cool who doesn't smoke or drink!"

I knew what that meant. I'd have to take risks if I wanted to be cool, so I experimented with smoking and drinking. Drugs were out. I didn't want to mess up my mind with dope. I choked and gagged over the cigarettes and could hardly swallow the booze. It didn't stop me though. I was determined to be cool like my brother.

After I was cool enough, I started hanging around my brother and his friends. I thought if I showed him how cool I was in daily life, I'd get him to like me. I failed. He didn't think I was cool and kept calling me a jerk. It seemed futile.

I wanted the groovy life he had and wanted him to think I was groovy, but I didn't succeed at it. I gave up and thought I'd make another attempt when I got older. Then if he gave me any trouble, I could beat him up. There wasn't much I could do while I was only ten.

After my failure to become cool, I returned to my former ways. I gave little attention to the family and they ignored me. After a period, my mother tried again with humanetics.

That time she used a different approach. Instead of saying, "I'm going to teach you humanetics," she gave us a choice. She said there would be meetings in our living room and anyone was welcome to attend. I wasn't doing anything at the time, so I told my mother I would come. She didn't apply any pressure, but she let me know she was happy and thought it was the thing I should do. By that time I was 11 and had quite a collection of problems. If humanetics could solve them, that would be just great.

Meeting time came but only a few family members showed up—my oldest sister, my mother, and I. At the meetings we learned about humanetics from tape-recorded lectures by Mr. Wetherill. We felt neither scolded nor belittled. We were just told the simple facts.

I learned that people have been using the wrong system of reasoning since birth. It is a system that is based on forming and obeying personal motives and is called the relative system. In that system everyone is a self-appointed judge of what he wants. Because his wants contradict, trouble tends to be rampant in his life.

Humanetics explained another system of reasoning: a system that frees people from trouble. It is the absolute system based on reality. It enables a person to avoid trouble by letting reality show him what he should do.

At first the idea of doing what I should do seemed disagreeable. I thought it would mean all work and no play. I thought I'd have to be a good little boy and do whatever my parents said.

My parents corrected that wrong impression. They said I should do whatever I thought was right. They said that the reality of my life was different from theirs; therefore, I would be the one who would know what action was right. They assured me they would not block any right action I thought I should take. They offered to point out any reality that was not clear, so I could make correct decisions.

We discussed the fundamental principle of humanetics, the law of absolute right. It states that right action gets right results and wrong action gets wrong results. My parents assured me that if I reasoned from the law of absolute right, they would not punish me. I'd get a wrong result every time I took wrong action and, therefore, would get punished by reality.

That had great appeal. As long as I studied humanetics, I could do anything I wanted without getting punished. Boy, was I wrong! Every time I did something I knew wasn't right, I got punished by reality just as they said.

One time I took a bicycle ride to escape from my chores. I rode down a steep hill, fell off, and came home with a lump on my head. My parents didn't need to punish me for running away from my chores. I got punished by the law of gravity, a piece of reality.

During a tape-recorded lesson, I learned about the command phrase technique. First I learned that command phrases are untrue statements we tell ourselves when we are emotional and our intelligence is reduced. Under that circumstance, we form or adopt command phrases because we make ourselves believe they are true. Thereafter we reason from them and act on them. As a result, they cause trouble.

Our command phrases express personal motives. Because we are intent on getting our way, we think we really want to carry out the irrational commands. That is a delusion. If we could see command phrases for what they are, we would never act on them.

I learned that command phrases don't disappear after we form them. They are stored in our unconscious minds for repeated use. We need to bring them up to the conscious level and see them for what they are. When we look at command phrases while we are calm, we can see that they are irrational and are not true; then they release. That is how a person uses the command phrase technique.

It looked like something I could use because I wanted to eliminate all my problems right away. I brought up command phrases but I still had my problems. My mother explained my mistake. I was using the command phrase technique to satisfy my motives. It doesn't work under that circumstance.

One thing I wanted was to make myself a better athlete by picking up command phrases. I wanted to be the best and make everybody jealous. Bringing up command phrases didn't improve my ability. The phrases didn't release because I had wrong intent. I wanted to satisfy my motive to be a better athlete, not to correct my wrong thinking and reason from reality. Sometimes I agreed with the phrases and wanted to reason from them. For instance, "If I'm a great athlete, I'll get everybody's attention."

What I didn't realize was that I had my attention on the wrong point. I wanted personal advantages and if the command phrase technique would provide them, I'd use it to change my thinking. But if reasoning from the command phrases of my motives seemed to provide advantages, I'd agree with them. I never got what I wanted so I was frustrated.

My frustration ended when I got my thinking out of the

groove of personal advantages and began to take right action. To take right action, I had to reason entirely from reality. To reason from reality, I had to take attention off myself and put it on reality. Then reality could dictate my action.

After I decided to take right action just because it was right, the command phrase technique began to work. Instead of eliminating problems for personal benefit, I let reality indicate what problems needed attention. Then I picked up command phrases simply to eliminate wrong thinking. The results were astonishing. For the first time in my life, I could eliminate trouble without causing another kind of trouble in its place. I saw that there was a way to solve my problems without running away from them.

At school I was able to maintain high grades with little effort, and I stopped being a compulsive TV watcher.

During that time I was going to Sunday School, and one day I told my teacher I was learning humanetics. A strange look came over her face. She seemed disapproving. She asked me if my mother knew. I said, "Yes, she is teaching me." She looked more disapproving. I was puzzled. Why wouldn't anyone be delighted to have people know about humanetics? It had enabled me to eliminate problems I had never been able to solve.

I continued going to meetings and learned more about humanetics. I learned there is a lot more to understand about applying the law of absolute right than merely stating that right action gets right results and wrong action gets wrong results.

When I had first heard about the law, I thought, "Oh, even I know that." But when I analyzed my past actions, I saw that I really hadn't known it. I remembered many times when I had taken action I had known was wrong. If I had understood the law of absolute right, I wouldn't have taken the wrong action.

By understanding the law, a person learns that everybody somehow causes his own trouble. That was very unpalatable to me. It was so disagreeable I opposed it right away and argued about it. It seemed ridiculous. If it were true, I had to face the fact that I brought my trouble on myself. Ugh! That meant I could no longer blame my trouble on anyone else.

My mind jumped to incidents involving my older brothers. They often punched me when I walked by. They hit me for what appeared to be no reason. I couldn't think of one thing I did to invite it. I felt like an innocent victim, so I asked my mother to explain how I caused that trouble. She gave me an answer I didn't like. She suggested I give up the idea I was the innocent little kid I thought I was. The law is right and if I had trouble, I caused it.

She gave me some command phrases I had installed that made me a target for their punches: "I'm their punching bag because I'm smaller." "I'll let them know I hate them even if I don't say a word." She said if I eliminated my command phrases, it wouldn't stop them from punching, but they would stop punching me. She said they had command phrases causing them to punch people, and I had command phrases inviting people to punch me.

I brought up command phrases such as, "Everyone picks on me." "No one leaves me alone." "They can't keep their hands off me." I noticed an immediate change. Soon my brothers weren't punching me anymore. I saw how I certainly did cause my own trouble. My command phrases had caused action on my part that had attracted the punches.

Since my oldest sister was learning humanetics at the same time, we started spending a lot of time together. That was unusual because she was four years older. Age alone had formerly been an impenetrable barrier between us. After humanetics, the age barrier broke down completely. We worked and played together without the usual brother-sister conflict. The small amount of conflict in our relationship was limited to occasional reactions to one another's behavior. When we noticed the emotion, we picked up command phrases and ended the conflict.

My relationships with the rest of the family began to change, too. We weren't yet a loving bunch of brothers and sisters, but the conflicts were greatly reduced.

In humanetics I learned that all conflict is wrong by definition because it indicates that personal motives are being reasoned from. I made a decision to eliminate conflict in all its forms. Whenever I noticed myself in conflict, it was easy to pull out because that was the right thing to do.

Not long after that, I met Mr. Wetherill. My mother had said he was different from any person I had met. She said, "Wait, you'll see." Well, I waited and, during my wait, I formed many judgments of him. I thought he'd be authoritative, a superhuman being possessed of many powers and a person in control.

My judgments were destroyed when I met him. He was different. He didn't have an air of authority nor seem superhuman nor was he a person who controlled. He was calm and peaceful, and I felt drawn to him immediately. The spectacular difference wasn't in his appearance; it was in his thinking and speaking. He didn't reason from motives like everybody else I had met. He reasoned from reality. Instead of acting on personal whims, he did what the situation called for. He did not try to control our minds. As a matter of fact, he told us not to believe what he said, but to observe the reality he was describing. Then we could reason from the reality itself, and not from his words. In that case, we wouldn't have to believe but would know.

The first really right relationship I ever had was with him.

It was based on reality and was devoid of conflict. I never dreamed that someday I'd have similar relationships with the members of my family.

About the same time, I met a pair of teenage twins who had been learning humanetics ever since they were five years old. I had never seen any brother and sister treat each other the way they did. They didn't fight nor have even one emotional blowup. I was amazed. I still was having some difficulty with my family, but they were the best of friends.

At times I asked the boy, "Don't you get mad at her? Doesn't she bug you?"

He always said, "No."

"How come?"

"Because I know I cause my problems and any trouble I get into, I can't blame on her. Anyway, I know she wouldn't hurt me."

Wow! I understood why he couldn't blame his trouble on her, but I didn't understand why he'd say, "She wouldn't hurt me."

Most of my brothers and sisters apparently wanted to hurt me and make me suffer.

It took awhile to see that when trouble arose between us, it was caused by contradictory motives. My brothers and sisters didn't really want to hurt me. They wanted to satisfy their motives, the same as I did, and because the motives contradicted, we got hurt.

The relationships among my oldest sister, my mother, my father, and me kept improving as we continued to study humanetics.

Meanwhile, the other members of the family were deep in problems. In fact, their problems were getting worse.

My next older brother's situation was especially bad. He was involved with a group of teenagers who were living the "fun way of life." That meant smoking, drinking, drugs, sex, and rebellion against authority. He offered me a chance to join, but I had fallen for that groovy life once before and had gotten into so much trouble I knew I'd better not try it again. He was surprised when I turned him down.

A few months later I was even more surprised when he got involved in humanetics. It was quick and unexpected. After my mother and sister talked to him about some of his problems, he changed. He stopped seeing his old friends. He stopped smoking, drinking, and taking drugs, not because he was told to stop but because he wanted to stop. He saw the flaw in his old way of life and adopted the new way.

After he got into humanetics, we started to see a lot more of each other. Formerly we had hated each other's guts, had avoided being together when we could. When our involvement in humanetics brought us together, some of our patterns of the past tended to continue. At first our relationship almost seemed to get worse. We had verbal conflicts and competed to excel in our understanding of humanetics. That blocked us. We used the command phrase technique to eliminate the competition and began to experience moments of nonconflict. That gave us a taste of what our relationship could become, and we knew we were moving in the right direction.

Soon my second oldest brother became interested. He was five years older, and because of the difference in our ages, we had hardly acknowledged each other's existence except for occasional name-calling.

My mother asked him to read the first book Mr. Wetherill had written about humanetics, and she helped him to understand it by discussing it with him. Before I knew what was happening, he also was attending meetings.

A large part of the family was then involved, and it was

working out well. Conflicts and problems of all sorts reduced tremendously. We were becoming a happy family. An important reason was that we had decided to eliminate all conflict as soon as we detected it. All that was needed was for one person to stop fighting and that ended a conflict. After all, it takes two to fight.

Most of the conflicts that were left resulted from misunderstandings. One time I was looking for my wallet. I searched and searched. I asked my little sister if she knew where it was. Automatically she jumped to the conclusion that I was accusing her of stealing it. She defended herself and attacked me. I started to defend myself, so we were in conflict. Each of us was trying to prove he was right and the other wrong. We dropped the fight. Humanetics had taught me there is no need for defense: You can't defend what's wrong and you don't need to defend what's right. Later I found the wallet in my coat pocket.

Our remaining conflicts stopped when we listened to each other with the intent to reason from reality in relation to whatever was being talked about. That took our minds off each other and eliminated our tendency to attack or defend. It made the misunderstandings easy to discover and correct.

We began to notice that some persons were opposing our involvement in humanetics. I couldn't understand why they would be opposing reality which is God's creation, but my grandmother was one of those persons. She opposed, ridiculed and discredited humanetics. She denied its validity. I was amazed. How could she deny the results that humanetics had accomplished in our family? We had ended an enormous amount of trouble.

My two older brothers and sister had lost their compulsions to smoke, drink, take drugs, involve themselves in sex activity, disobey laws, vandalize, fight, and associate with kids

Stopping Family Fights

who did such things. Besides, we had all stopped our terrible fighting at home. Our parents no longer needed to discipline us because reality was in control. Our wrong action had brought wrong results, and we had gotten the message.

No matter what we said, my grandmother still opposed humanetics. She claimed our changes came from God. We agreed that a humanetics correction comes from God. We explained that God created reality and that the law of absolute right is a part of reality. We said that humanetics describes a reality that has been overlooked.

My grandmother was trying to tell us that it was through prayer and the church that our family had changed. It wasn't. Our family had been praying and going to church during all our lives while we were fighting. Our study of humanetics enabled us to change.

The greatest changes came when we used the relationship technique. That technique eliminates hurt feelings, grudges and hooks between people. It establishes a relationship based on reality. It shows why right relationships can't exist in the relative system: Motives are barriers between people, and in the relative system, people all reason from their motives.

I think the most startling change for me was in my relationship with my older brother. We were still having problems and we both knew it. Our conversations still contained subtle digs that were meant to discredit, and we both felt the hurts that resulted.

Mr. Wetherill applied the right relationship technique by asking us to look into each other's eyes with no motives. I looked at him carefully. He seemed entirely different. I realized that in the past I had seen him through a screen of personal motives. I had judged him and had then based my thinking on the judgments rather than on reality.

Mr. Wetherill asked me to remember the worst thing he

had done. My mind jumped back through several incidents and stopped at one when we were both small. I was playing with my favorite truck on our coffee table. He saw me. He took my truck and asked if he could play with it.

I said, "Yes, if you don't break it."

While playing, he knocked it off the table and it broke. I had held that against him ever since. Other incidents in which he had hurt my feelings came to mind. I was shocked to see that the long-forgotten past could have had so much effect on our present relationship.

After Mr. Wetherill asked my brother to do the same thing, he said, "Those incidents from the past don't matter anymore. Each person is different now. You no longer want to hurt each other nor be the one who comes out on top. You can drop your grudges and begin a new life together, based on a right relationship."

I could see that the hurts I had been holding against my brother had been caused by the contradictions between our personal motives, and not between us. That made it easy to drop the hurts. Then we were asked to remember some of the hooks we had used to obligate each other.

"See how you tried to get the other person to like you by special favors, extra attention and compliments. Remember how hurt you were when he didn't accept your hooks. See how your favors caused as much frustration as your conflicts. Let go of the hooks and let go of the hurts. Your obligation is not to a person but to reality. Basing relationships on reality is what works. When two persons are both reasoning from reality, they are unable to get into conflict with each other.

"You don't need to hold grudges nor sink hooks into each other. As you drop grudges and hooks, you will see that each of you really loves the other."

I thought back to when I had wanted him to think I was

cool and had tried to be like him. I saw the hooks I had tried to use, and when he refused the hooks, I was hurt and had held it against him. It was a relief to drop all such influences from the past. I dropped emotional tension I had not formerly been aware of. We hugged each other and shed some tears.

After that experience, our relationship was entirely different. Now I truly love my brother and enjoy his company. It is a relief to know we will never fight again.

I also went through the relationship technique with my mother, my sister and other brother. It was really great to get to know them. After that, our part of the family had no conflicts, and we were a truly loving unit. But there were other members of the family I didn't yet know. There was my father, who had gone along with humanetics in the beginning, in a superficial way, but had never made a basic reversal of approach to life by successfully adopting reality as his sole basis of reasoning. He wanted to satisfy his motives and retain his freedom to be wrong. As a result, he separated himself from humanetics and from the family.

Maybe someday he'll drop his motives and rejoin us. We don't hold anything against him; we love him and always will.

I didn't know my little sister either. I was very jealous of her before humanetics. She got most of my parents' attention and I resented it. Now she is studying humanetics, and, though she is quite young, she is making changes. My relationship with her has improved greatly. The jealousy seems to be gone. I understand my resentment of her. When she was born, I immediately disliked her because I was no longer the baby of the family. I was told to be a big boy and take care of myself. I didn't want to. I felt rejected and blamed it on her. Because of this misunderstanding, our relationship had been a disaster.

Then there was my oldest brother. He was so much older that I rarely spoke to him. We shared a bedroom. He slept on the bottom bunk and I slept on the top. Mostly we ignored each other. He worked long hours and that meant he wasn't able to do chores such as cleaning his room. That left me. I thought I had enough to do around the house without cleaning his half of our room and blamed my frustration on him for not being around to help.

There were many other grudges I held against him. He had been our baby-sitter, and I hated him for beating me up and playing practical jokes and for scores of other things. All those grudges were dropped after he began studying humanetics and we went through the right relationship technique. Now we spend time together, work together and discuss our problems. I can give him information. Can you imagine that? A teenager explaining anything to his brother who is eight years older! What a thrill! He tells me things, too, and there are no barriers between us.

Humanetics brought about many dramatic changes in our family. It wiped out virtually all our conflict and provided a solution for our remaining problems. It changed our family from arch enemies into true friends.

At the time of this writing, we no longer live in a large house where we'd had plenty of room to escape from each other. Instead, we live in a three-bedroom apartment and we love it. We are a large family of persons who have learned to live together successfully and in peace.

My relationships with other members of the family are so different that no one seems to be the same person anymore. We understand and love each other. We would never knowingly hurt each other, so if a hurt is felt, we find and eliminate the wrong thinking that caused it.

My three brothers and I share a bedroom. We don't get in each other's way; it works just fine. We don't need the privacy of separate rooms. We don't have secrets to keep from each other because we trust each other. We feel safe.

Why? What happened? What caused the sudden change in our family? What stopped the conflicts and solved our problems? Was it church? School? Government? Authorities? Discipline? Nope. In one way or another, we had tried them all and they had failed.

It was our study of humanetics that gave us the basic facts about human behavior and told us how to stop the family fights.

The Devil Made Me Do It

DID YOU ever feel as if you had a tiny devil perched on your shoulder whispering suggestions in your ear? "Go on, buy it. It'll make you look terrific" or "It'll taste delicious, eat it" or "I'll show them who's boss" and so on.

Until I joined our behavioral research group, giving attention to my thinking was as foreign to me as reading the score of a symphony is to a small child. I thought I was free to think what I pleased as long as I bridled my tongue and did not act too far out of line. It was my involvement in our research group that enabled me to see how I'd programmed myself in unguarded moments for behavior that I jokingly blamed on the devil.

My urges to spend money kept me broke from payday to payday, and most of my pay was spent on clothes. Like a lamb to the slaughter, I followed the fashion trends until my closets were bulging and my credit exhausted. Try as I might, I could not resist a trip through the petite section of every clothing store I entered.

When I learned about how my judgments gave me urges to buy compulsively, I knew I could get that buying monkey off my back. One of the techniques I learned had me list on paper all the thoughts that came to mind to cause my shopping sprees.

"No matter what I spend, I never have enough of anything." "Buying clothes makes me feel good." "Shopping is one of my greatest pleasures." "I have to keep buying until I find the perfect outfit." There were many more ideas I had allowed to motivate me, going back to childhood when I'd played dress up with clothes in the attic and cut up the mail-order catalog to dress my paper doll.

It was a real surprise to learn that judgments formed over the years were still lodged in my unconscious mind and that they were the cause of my compulsive behavior. Even though I was surprised, I could also see the evidence that the information was correct.

Almost immediately, I used the command phrase technique to raise judgment after judgment to the conscious level, and my behavior changed. No longer was I a sucker for advertising gimmicks and my compulsions to separate me from my money. I could make logical decisions about when and on what to spend money.

More important, I don't have to blame my crazy behavior on the devil anymore because I realize I do it to myself.

Relationships

AS FAR BACK as I can remember, I was Mommy's girl. I adored her and demanded her constant attention. I recall following her by the hour from room to room, recounting every story of the day and insisting that she hear every one in detail. She was patient with my demands and usually responded with great interest. If she happened to look away from me to check on the meat or sweep the floor, I could hardly stand it.

"You're not listening to me!" I would exclaim.

Strangely enough she always seemed to have listened, because she could repeat everything I had said for the preceding few minutes, including the most minute details. I thought she was wonderful.

Every night before I went to sleep, she sat on the edge of my bed and sang to me. I loved it and begged for more. This nightly ritual was an understood requirement in our relationship. It made me feel secure and comfortable. I used her like a human sleeping pill to put my mind at rest.

Throughout my childhood, I was bothered with sicknesses and little physical problems. Whenever I became ill, I was sure to be treated like a queen. My mother waited on me hand and foot. She often brought meals to my bed, propped the pillows behind me, and talked with me cheerfully to lift my spirits.

I began to like getting sick and found it a convenient way to escape from household chores and other activities I'd rather avoid. It was fun to have a person at my beck and call. Another benefit, I thought, was watching the jealousy it evoked in my big brother. He was robust and rarely received such royal treatment.

Getting sick also had its disadvantages. One day my mother informed me that I would have to be hospitalized for a week. My heart sank. The thought of doctors and nurses and drugs was scary enough to contemplate, but leaving Mommy was the most frightening part of all.

She visited me as frequently as the hospital permitted and attempted to distract me as best she could. As long as she was there, I felt calm and secure; but the minute she had to leave, I went into a panic. "Don't leave me!" I'd choke through my tears.

Sometimes my physical problems took the form of accidents. I can remember doing things like stubbing my toe while playing with my friends and carefully concealing the fact that it hurt as I bravely hobbled home. The moment I saw my mother and my friends were out of sight, I would burst into tears and act as though the pain were excruciating. Despite my antics, she always acted concerned and quickly administered the necessary first aid.

I wasn't willing to share the attention she gave me. My heaviest competition was a few children she watched during the day. I didn't like those little "intruders" and thought they were brats. It seemed that every time I wanted her attention, one of them got there first. She responded to them with the same kind of enthusiasm she showed me. The kids loved her and sometimes cried when their mothers came to take them home. I wanted to kill them. They had no right to come into my house, use my things and take my mother away from me.

In a fit of jealousy I tried to destroy a record of mine that they listened to incessantly. I grabbed it and scraped it with my fingernails as hard as I could. After I finished, the darn thing played just as well as it had the day it was bought!

At a young age, I had aspired to be a teacher. These kids seemed to be perfect little guinea pigs. So I lined them up on chairs in my room and sat facing them with a pen and paper. If one of them slipped by forgetting to raise his hand, I gave him a check. If he protested, I gave him another check. I loved the feeling of power that tingled in my fingertips with each mark I made. Then I heard that one of my students had gone crying to his mother because I had given him so many checks! I don't remember playing teacher after that.

Because I was much smaller than my brother, I sought my mother's protection any way that I could. When he happened to poke me while playing a game, I screamed, "Ben hit me!" My mother ran to my rescue and gave him the deserved punishment while I sat back and gloated. I even remember being hit by him and then hitting my mother in the same place so that she'd know how it felt.

"He went like that!" I'd exclaim as I delivered the appropriate punch. She just stood there and let me do it. In fact, both of my parents almost never did anything more extreme than spanking us. So I thought I could get away with a lot.

One day after Ben and I got into a spat, I started screaming bloody murder. My dad got so upset that he slapped him across the face. I was shocked. That had never happened before. And Ben had hardly touched me. I felt guilty and ashamed, but it didn't prevent me from going into my screaming act on later occasions.

My mother had told me about how poor she was when she was young and how she was going to give us all the advantages she had been deprived of as a child. I always seemed to be taking lessons of some sort to add culture to my life—ballet, piano, drama, swimming, and even roller-skating. No matter how many activities I was involved in, I wanted more. My appetite for new things was insatiable.

I remember the excitement I experienced at Christmastime when we decorated the tree with special ornaments. My mother made Christmas candy and eggnog. My brother wrapped my presents in the bedroom with my mother while I stayed outside the closed door. Then I wrapped his gifts with her while he waited in anticipation. My parents would stay up for hours making something special for us and adding all the finishing touches so Christmas would be "just perfect."

On Christmas morning we would awaken at six o'clock and try to force our parents out of bed. After we had emptied our stockings of the goodies and opened all the presents, I could never manage to say, "Thank you, I love them all." Instead, I'd look around the room and ask, "Is that all?" Then I'd carefully count all of my gifts to be sure that I had received just as many as my brother.

As I grew older and entered junior high school, I noticed my friends' attitude toward their parents had changed. They seemed to think parents were repulsive and gross. They were embarrassed to be seen with them and acted as though they hardly existed. Soon, I started treating my parents the same way. I certainly didn't want to look weird, so I conformed to my friends' thinking and found that I, too, felt repelled by my parents.

I was afraid to be affectionate because I knew my friends would think I was strange and uncool. I decided I wouldn't touch my parents if I could avoid it. After all, I was 13 years old now, and wasn't that old enough to start running my own life? It was time for me to grow up and show how cool I was, and kissing Mommy was no way to be cool.

If I happened to be shopping with my mother, I was afraid my friends would see us so I'd walk a few paces behind her so that we wouldn't be seen together. At times I was surprised at these actions myself, but my friends' opinions mattered more. I wanted them to accept me, and hating your parents seemed to be one of the major requirements.

I often felt very confused about my thinking. Half of me wanted to grow up, and half of me wanted to stay a child. I sometimes wanted my parents to be affectionate, but I couldn't get myself to warm up to them. So I held myself back and tried my best to fit in with my peers.

It was around that time that my mother began to speak to me about humanetics. She had been studying the information in an effort to discover the meaning in life that she had been searching for. Because of humanetics, she had been learning to deal with life in a new way without emotional turmoil. Although I had noticed changes in her as a result, I was afraid to get too interested. At least, not yet.

I learned about command phrases and how they control a person's behavior.

They were described as pieces of irrational thinking a person installs into his unconscious mind while emotional. I began to recognize command phrases in other people's conversations and noticed how they influenced their behavior. I learned how command phrases could be brought up to the conscious level without emotion and lose their control over a person's thinking. I liked bringing up command phrases and found it very easy. I even attended some beginners' classes on humanetics for a few months. But again, I was afraid of getting too interested and didn't want my friends to discover what I was involved in.

When my mother spoke with me about humanetics, I assumed she was trying to mold me into the image of a perfect daughter. It was obvious that I wasn't fitting the picture and that it would take a lot of pressure on her part for those changes to become real. The more pressure she applied for me to listen, the more I resisted. I had my own life to live, and sometimes I challenged her just for the sake of displaying my rebellion.

Despite my resistance, there were times when the meaning of her words came clear in my mind. She spoke of the concept that everyone causes his own trouble. Although that went down hard, I saw a glimmer of truth in the idea.

One time when my brother and I were blaming somebody for something he had done, she said that when a person is pointing his finger at someone else, he should turn the finger around and point it at himself. In other words, he should look at his own input to the trouble and not blame others for it. As she spoke, my brother and I looked at each other with amazement as though a light had suddenly lit in our minds. "Neat!" we both exclaimed.

For a fleeting moment, I saw something that provided a solution to the trouble I was in. But I was too busy with my own life to pursue it any further; I just let it slip away.

In the years that followed, adjusting to high school became more and more painful. I wanted to be popular, but I was afraid of sex involvements. I wanted a boyfriend, but I didn't have the necessary "equipment" to attract one. I wanted to be smart, but I didn't want to be ridiculed. I felt confused and frustrated almost all the time.

Even though I was trying to project the image of a rebellious teenager, I also had a lot of moralistic thinking that I was afraid to drop. When I found out that my best girlfriend talked about going skinny-dipping with some boys, I was horrified. The next day I told her I wasn't going to hang around with her anymore, and I went searching elsewhere for friends I could trust.

Soon I was involved with a group of kids who were avid

churchgoers. Even though I had almost no religious background, I agreed to join them at a summer church camp.

During my stay at the camp, I was approached by a girl who tried to convert me. She started interrogating me about my religious life. "Do you love Jesus? Have you let Him into your heart?" The more demanding she became, the more confused I felt. "Have you given your life to Jesus?" I kept mumbling, "I don't know, I don't know." Finally she stopped the interrogation and told me she'd go pray for me. I'd been praying she'd leave me alone. I escaped to my cabin to avoid any more "converters" that might be on the loose.

As I was lying in bed, my mind went in circles. What's wrong with these people? They seemed so hypocritical, so full of double standards. While at camp, they were sneaking boys into their cabins and ditching chapel service. I knew that some of them lied to their parents, sneaked whiskey, and had stolen a car to go joyriding. And they were supposed to be worshipping Jesus? How could they justify their wrong behavior? Didn't they know what was right? And what about me? Did I know what was right? Is there an escape from all these contradictions? My mind seemed to spin out of control.

Suddenly my thinking slowed down. My thoughts began to clarify. I realized that the answers had been there all along. They were right there in the things my mother had been saying to me that I had been trying so hard to avoid. The idea of being right just because it was right was beginning to make sense for the first time. I realized that she really hadn't been trying to give me a hard time. She had just been attempting to give me the information because she knew it would solve the problems I had been trapped in. Suddenly I began to see an escape from these problems. And it had been there all along in the information of humanetics.

I could see that my friends were crazy, and I had been

crazy, too. I wanted to understand what the purpose of my life really was, and I had a sudden desire to be right. I hardly knew what was happening in my mind, but I knew it felt different.

The next day during chapel service, we were asked to pass a cup around the group which was symbolic of the cup of life. We were to state with what we desired to fill this cup. As I grasped the cup in my hands, I found myself thinking about humanetics again. The evidence of its correctness seemed so clear in my mind. Before I knew what I was saying, the words came out, "I want to fill my life with the desire to do what is right and not to follow my personal wants." I could hardly believe I had said it, but I knew it was right. Afterward, I felt a peaceful calm inside. I knew this was a new beginning for me.

After I returned home, I told my mother about the incident in the chapel. The next thing I knew, I was invited to meet Mr. Wetherill, who developed humanetics.

I wasn't sure I was ready for this. Everything seemed to be happening so fast. What would he be like? What should I say?

As we approached the place where I was to meet him, my anxiety mounted. I told my mother that I didn't have to meet him; I could jump out of the car right now. She just drove on.

Instead of just introducing himself and saying a few words, he talked to me for three hours. What transpired during that conversation caused me to realize what great misunderstandings I had harbored about life itself. He spoke of a brother and sister who had eliminated their quarreling when they stopped blaming trouble on each other and began to realize that each of them had brought it on himself. I listened with amazement that such a relationship could be possible. I wanted to learn more because my brother and I had such a painful relationship. I wondered if that could change.

The more he spoke, the more I realized how wrong I

had been to treat my mother the way I had. I had been so cruel and heartless, so selfish and uncaring. I wanted to change. I wanted her to know I really loved her and that I hadn't realized what I was doing. I was sorry for the times I had resisted when she tried to give me information about humanetics. And I was sorry for the treatment I had subjected her to in my peaks of rebellion.

In the middle of the conversation, she walked into the room. I jumped up and threw my arms around her. This was the first time I had hugged her in years. I felt tears streaming down my face as I held her close. I was so sorry, so desperate to make up for the hurts that had been inflicted.

Then Mr. Wetherill asked us to sit facing each other and look into each other's eyes. He said we had never really known each other; all we had known were the judgments we had formed of each other. Because we had kept piling judgment on top of judgment, we weren't able to contact the real person underneath. This had caused us to hurt each other without awareness. I began to realize that I had never really looked at my mother without making a judgment.

I could see how I had used and abused her. I felt as though I had met her for the first time in my life. It was great!

Suddenly we could talk freely and openly. I felt as though I were her friend and not her daughter. In fact, she was a better friend than any of my peers. I no longer felt the tremendous embarrassment about her being my mother and found that I actually enjoyed her company. We talked as we had in my childhood.

The generation gap seemed to be dissolving before our eyes. Because she no longer fell into the category of a mother, it seemed natural for me to address her by her first name, Betty. We didn't have to play the conventional mother-daughter roles of the past. We were real friends.

It was becoming obvious to me that there was a marked disparity between the relationship we shared and the ones I observed between my friends and their mothers. They seemed to hate their mothers with a passion. I realized that I, too, had felt the same way and would have continued to despise her if it weren't for this change.

Humanetics was providing a new communication between us. Our interests in life were merging rather than separating. We were now concerned about each other's welfare and were eager to drop the former hurts rather than create new ones. Because our relationship had undergone such a striking change, I wanted to protect it any way I could. If a misunderstanding arose, I tried to work it out immediately.

My friends didn't seem to care if they hurt their mothers; they tried to avoid communicating with them as much as possible. They weren't interested in working out misunderstandings; they didn't care to improve matters. I was so grateful to humanetics for removing the grudges and pain and giving us an opportunity to have the relationship we had always wanted.

During the next few years, I attended regular meetings of the study group to which my mother belonged. Then an opportunity arose for me to move across the country to work closely with the humanetics research group. I was very excited about the prospect. I had visited there a year before and had worked with a group of teenagers. I loved working with them because I had had so little contact with others my age in humanetics. I not only longed for friends in humanetics, but I had also fantasized about having a boyfriend who was involved in it. I had already picked out just the guy I was looking for. I had met Charles on the previous visit and thought we had hit it off pretty well.

Although I wanted to believe that my excitement over

the prospect of moving was because of my desire to study humanetics, I was really more interested in developing a close relationship with him. If I had been aware of what was going on in my mind, I would have realized that the painful craving and tingling anticipation I had felt about seeing him were definitely not excitement about studying humanetics.

As the time for the move approached, I was caught in the middle of two contradictions. I couldn't wait to arrive there, but I was also terribly frightened about leaving Betty. It was as though I were suddenly being thrust back into the childhood scene of leaving Mommy to go into the hospital. But this time, it was for more than a week.

Contemplating the finality of the move, thoughts whirled through my mind in rapid succession: "I can't take this." "I'll never see her again." "I have to have her near me." "I'll never be able to make it on my own." The more I entertained these thoughts, the more emotional I felt.

In retrospect I realize that I had been thinking through command phrases much like the ones I had installed as a child in that original hospital scene. But I didn't understand what was happening then. All I knew was that I was emotional and confused.

Instead of using my intelligence to examine this emotion, I just aggravated the situation by roaming about the house, haunted by nostalgia from my childhood. I had never lived anywhere else and felt painfully attached to the place as though I would be leaving part of myself behind.

As we drove across the country, I went through hell. I had frequent pains near my heart, and my legs felt weak. I couldn't sleep and didn't feel like eating. I wondered if I were going to die. I tried to bring up command phrases, but that didn't help. I had already learned that the phrases have to be brought up in the absence of emotion, but I couldn't let go of the emotion long enough to have the corrections take place.

Later I discovered that what I had been experiencing was not connected with my heart, and that it was most likely nothing more than a bad case of gas!

When I arrived at my new home, I felt like a nervous wreck, so full of excitement and anxiety that I could hardly function. Almost immediately, I felt disappointed. I had expected that one of my friends would run up and throw her arms around me in a joyous welcome. When I arrived, she was seated on the couch with a sprained ankle!

As the months wore on, my unhappiness increased. I found life wasn't fulfilling my fantasies. Charles was getting very friendly with another girl in the research group. In fact she was getting very chummy with a lot of the friends I had acquired on my first visit. How dare she butt into my territory! These were my friends.

Sometimes I just sat there and glared at her when she seemed to be flirting with Charles. Then I'd let him have it with a strong dose of the silent treatment until he asked me what was wrong. I'd pout and bitch and let him know I didn't like the attention he gave her. Soon he'd try to make up to me by giving me the special attention I craved.

During this period, I was depressed most of the time. I called Betty frequently and sometimes cried from my unhappiness. I wanted her sympathy and comfort.

Although other people tried to help me with my distress, they couldn't seem to get their points across. They tried to point out the ways I was bringing the trouble on myself. I knew intellectually that everybody causes his own trouble, but I couldn't relate it to the agony I was facing. I was sure that if circumstances were different and if people stopped blocking me, life would certainly be perfect, and I would be able to have that desired relationship and really make it work. The more people tried to help, the more I resisted. I didn't want their help. I just wanted what I wanted.

During this period I was attending humanetics meetings regularly and attempting to apply the information with little success. My understanding was only superficial and I failed to apply it in my daily experiences. I knew that humanetics was correct, but I didn't know if I could make the required changes.

Mr. Wetherill began talking about "hooks" and the crippling effect they had on relationships. He described them as tools a person uses to pull others close to him in an effort to acquire influence and control. I realized that I had many hooks in Betty, but the thought of dropping them was very frightening. I thought it might destroy our relationship totally. How could I love her if I didn't try to pull her close? And what about the relationship with Charles? The only thing that kept us attracted to each other was the hooks we had both sunk so deeply. The thought of completely dropping them was too terrifying to consider.

As my anxiety mounted, I had increasing difficulty sleeping. Sometimes I'd roll around for hours worrying about anything that came into my mind. I worried about Betty. I worried about my problems and frustrations. I fantasized about the life I wanted in which I was the center of the universe and everything else revolved around me. Every time I brought up a command phrase, I found myself agreeing with it instead of dropping it.

During this state of confusion, I became more and more crippled in my studies of humanetics.

Then I learned of a prospective visit from Betty. I was ecstatic. I could hardly wait to see her again and bask in the glory of her love.

During her stay, we spent as much time together as we could. We talked together about our troubles and gossiped about the people in the group about whom we shared

Relationships 111

mutual judgments. It felt good to be with her again, knowing that we could depend on each other not to discuss these feelings with anybody else.

Yet mixed in with this warm feeling was a kind of tension I didn't understand. I suddenly found myself eating compulsively out of nervous anxiety. Because the hooks had been so strong, I was constantly worried about what she was thinking of me and fearful that I might do something that she'd disapprove of. Moreover, I couldn't really enjoy her company because of the terrifying fear of the separation soon to befall us.

When the time arrived to say good-bye, I hugged her and cried. After she left, the pain haunted me. It was as though I had been high on a drug and were suffering withdrawal symptoms.

All during this period, I was listening to more information about humanetics from Mr. Wetherill. I still tried to apply what I heard but found I couldn't. He spoke of the difference between the personal plan and the natural plan. He described the personal plan as one in which a person reasons from fantasies about how he wants his life to unfold, and frustrates himself in a fruitless effort to make those fantasies come true.

I knew I had entertained many fantasies, but I had a nagging feeling that the fantasies really could be fulfilled and that my personal plan could indeed work. He described the natural plan as one in which a person just receives what comes in his life and does what he thinks he should with no desire to control the outcome.

I knew there was some gap in my reasoning, something I needed to understand, but I couldn't determine what the missing key might be.

One night, Mr. Wetherill met with a group of us as he

did every week. The conversation began in the usual way with my attempt to listen through an undercurrent of resistance. Then something very different happened.

He began to speak about a trance that a person is born into. The trance insulates him from everybody and surrounds him like a bubble. In this trance he believes everything should work out in his life. It causes him to imagine unrealistic things about himself and to expect unrealistic things from others.

As he spoke, I felt as though I was awakening from a horrible nightmare and a deep sleep at the same time. Suddenly I could understand why I had been so miserable. I had been in a trance! It had made me believe crazy things about myself that weren't true. It had caused me to create fantastic pictures of what my life should be like. No wonder I had felt so hurt when people didn't give me the special attention I had thought I deserved.

I realized that in the past I had effectively hypnotized myself when people had told me I was pretty or talented or intelligent. I then acted on those suggestions as though they were real. Although no one had actually hypnotized me by putting me in a deep sleep, the emotion I experienced when they told me those things was enough to allow me to install their remarks as command phrases in my unconscious mind. When people said that I should be a model or a folksinger, I bought the idea. Later I began to act as though I were one, without realizing what had occurred in my mind.

I began to see the trance as something that had successfully kept me locked in a dreamworld of my own imagining. Because of the trance, I had equated happiness with something that substantiated my delusions. When I didn't get the support for those delusions, I was crushed.

Suddenly, I could understand why I had craved a relationship with a guy who would treat me like a queen. I had wanted to pull him into my trance and make him live with me in my dreamworld. I could see how impossible that would be. It just wouldn't work.

As I lay in bed that night, my whole life seemed to unfold in a flash right in front of me. I realized I had spent it inside this bubble, practically oblivious to the real world around me. For the first time, I was beginning to understand what life was all about.

The next morning, I felt like a new person. I wasn't depressed. I wasn't homesick. I wasn't miserable. I hardly knew myself! I just felt happy, really happy. I felt free and light. Everything looked so new and different to me. Even the people looked different. They weren't out to hurt me or make me feel jealous. Only my trance had been responsible for those feelings.

I didn't feel a void or a craving for something that would never be fulfilled.

When I entered my apartment, it looked different to me. Instead of a place where I was staying as a guest, it just looked like home. I realized that I had been in a trance about the idea of home itself. In my trance, home was the place I grew up and had become attached to. Suddenly home just seemed like a place where I lived and nothing more.

When I returned to my job the next day, it didn't seem like a chore as it had formerly. It just seemed like something I was supposed to do. It didn't even feel like work. Suddenly I loved doing it. I even surprised myself when I discovered that I was more interested in doing the job than in getting diverted. Formerly I had looked for any diversions I could to escape my duties. I realized that the trance had made me resist anything that didn't support it. I was beginning to understand what Mr. Wetherill had meant when he said that duty and desire should become one. I suddenly felt as though I wanted to do what I should do.

I found my intelligence was turning on in an exciting and unexpected way. I was not only able to put my mind on humanetics, but I also had a desire to learn as much as I could about it. I was beginning to see solutions to problems that had formerly seemed unsolvable. I found I was less dependent on people and more willing to take initiative. I was less interested in escaping into balm and more interested in looking for reality. Formerly reality had seemed harsh, cold and mysterious. I realized that through my trance, I had never known what reality was because the trance had effectively filtered reality from my view.

For years Mr. Wetherill had used the word "reality" and referred to it as the situation in front of a person that calls for specific action. I realized that my mind had been so cluttered with delusions and fantasies that I hadn't been able to see what reality called for. My trance had called for activities that supported it, like playing guitar for hours, scheming ways to be alone with Charles and listening to rock music. The trance had made those activities seem fascinating.

I was so excited about the change in my thinking that I wrote a letter to Betty explaining what had opened up in my mind. When I later spoke with her on the phone, she seemed very pleased. She told me I sounded different. She seemed different to me, too. She didn't seem to be the only person I could turn to anymore. I was developing new relationships now with lots of people who could provide help when I needed it. I realized how I had been using Betty as balm to salve my wounds. Now that those wounds were healing, I didn't need her to comfort me. Instead of feeling homesick, I felt happy to be where I was and to do what I was doing.

I didn't tell her that I didn't miss her anymore. I wasn't

sure she would understand. I was simply beginning to love her in a new way. I didn't feel like using her as a security blanket, because I was beginning to feel real security.

Then something happened.

With the new perspective of life that I was seeing, I found that I couldn't support some of the former thinking we had shared in our relationship. In the past I had been willing to be sympathetic and understanding with Betty, knowing that she would reciprocate. I could no longer justify that behavior because I saw the fallacy in it.

Suddenly our phone conversations became awkward and stilted. We didn't seem to have as much to say to each other. Sometimes she'd say "The reason I can't do anything right is because I'm so stupid."

Formerly I had shared such thinking and considered myself a failure, but I was beginning to understand how everybody feels like a failure when he tries to work his personal plan. It isn't because he has personally failed. It's because personal plans disregard reality, so they are unworkable. The trance I had been trapped in had deluded me into thinking that my plan would indeed materialize the way I had imagined. I realized that Betty was caught in a similar trance and that humanetics provided escape from it.

At times I became so concerned about her emotional thinking that I practically yelled at her over the phone so that she would wake up from her trance.

I had also shared those misunderstandings, but everything looked different now. Humanetics no longer appeared to be an interference in my effort to get my own way. Rather it was just a perfect explanation of how impossible it is to get it.

Several months earlier, a remarkable change had taken place in the children of the parents who were involved in the research group. Since the children were there because of their parents' interest, they attended the meetings with little idea as to what humanetics was all about. They were often bored and distracted during Mr. Wetherill's talks. They seemed to regard humanetics as an obstacle in their search for fun and excitement.

A private school had been set up for the purpose of providing an environment of rationality for the children. However, they weren't interested in being rational. They kept encountering one frustration after another because of their determination to follow their urges.

Because of their insistence on getting their own way, the children kept flouting the behavioral law. Instead of success, they found consistent failure: put-downs from their peers, discipline from their parents and teachers, jealousies of each other, and even physical fights.

Then one day something surprising happened. One of the children "spilled the beans." She told about how the kids had done some shoplifting and stealing from their mothers' purses. Everybody was shocked. She was petrified. What would the kids do to her now? Would they ever be her friends again? Would they forgive her?

When Mr. Wetherill learned about their wrong behavior, he gave them a choice. They either had to change their behavior and conform to right action, or they would lose their school. They were afraid of right action, but they were more afraid of losing their school.

Even though the girl who told was scared, she changed. She had no idea what would happen to her, but she knew that changing was right.

One day she saw one of the girls taking wrong action. She said, "I can't support you in what you're doing." The other girl was stunned, yet she was glad and stopped the action immediately.

Soon, one by one, each of the kids reflected her behavior and made the same basic change from supporting wrong action to supporting right action. When wrong action was observed, it was pointed out—sometimes by the teachers but more often by the kids themselves.

The changes in those children were remarkable. Unprecedented! I admired them for their courage and perseverance, yet I wondered if I had the guts to tell someone about his wrong action.

Because of my concern about Betty, I spoke with several people about the problem. In the past I hadn't wanted to talk with anyone about her problems because of my supposed loyalty. But I knew that such loyalty was simply a form of cruelty.

Then I learned of a prospective visit from my family. I felt excited and frightened at the same time. I wanted to see them, but I didn't know what to expect. When I spoke with Betty about it, she seemed apprehensive, too.

When she arrived, the tension between us was great. She looked stiff and uptight. Instead of giving her attention, I found myself hanging around my brother's girlfriend who was visiting along with them.

Betty seemed to be annoyed by this. I wanted to apologize for the misunderstandings we had encountered, yet I knew there was nothing to apologize about because the misunderstandings didn't need to be worked out. They just needed to be dropped.

After a couple of weeks, the rest of my family returned home while Betty stayed on. One night we were alone in the apartment where she had been staying. The atmosphere was very tense, so I kept the conversation superficial. We looked at some pictures, talked about some clothes she had bought and carefully avoided anything that might be explosive.

When the well of superficialities ran dry, she blurted, "I feel as though we don't have anything to talk about."

I asked, "What do you mean?"

She said, "It seems as though you can't talk to me."

Her eyes began to dart around, and she was on the verge of tears. Her emotion mounted as she began a series of irrational statements about how everybody was talking about her behind her back.

At this point she couldn't look at me. She started to cry. It was as though she were pulling on her last hook in a frantic effort to pull me over to her side. I told her I wasn't going to stop telling others about her problems if I thought they could help. In the past we had supported each other by hiding our problems from others, but I wasn't willing to do that anymore.

Even though I was trembling, the words kept pouring out of my mouth, "I can't support your wrong action anymore!"

She looked terrified. I felt shocked. I could hardly believe I had said it and decided to go back to my apartment.

When I left her that night, I had no idea what would happen. Perhaps she'd take the first plane home, and I'd never see her again.

She later told me that she was so angry after I left that she screamed to God at the top of her lungs. She considered leaving. She felt as though everybody on earth had abandoned her, including her own daughter. She felt pinned in a corner and knew she was forced to make a choice. If she kept on thinking the same way, she might go crazy.

When I saw her the next night at a meeting, I was still full of apprehension. I had no idea what might have taken place in her mind in the last 24 hours.

Mr. Wetherill's talk that night related to the idea of how important it is for people to refuse to support wrong action in others. He described a force inside people that makes them think and do what is wrong. This force needs to be frustrated so that it loses its control and gives people the free-

Relationships 119

dom to do what is right. The way to frustrate it is to refuse to support it in yourself and in others.

After Mr. Wetherill finished his talk, there was a discussion. Betty raised her hand. "Something very important has happened to me," she began.

As soon as I heard her voice, I knew things were different. She went on to say that the night before, she was having an emotional attack in which this force inside her was very strong and rebellious. She said that when I wouldn't support her in what she was saying, she had become very frustrated. But it was the force inside that was frustrated, not she. Later when she realized what had happened, she was glad that I had refused to support her outburst.

As she spoke, I felt so relieved that I wanted to burst into cheers. She had finally seen the reality and stopped the fight. I wanted to jump up and shout, "Right on, Mom! You tell 'em!"

She had finally surrendered. Not to Mr. Wetherill, not to me, not to any person. She had surrendered to the reality that she would never get her fantasized way. She had decided to let reality have its way. I knew that her struggle was over and everything would seem different to her now.

Later that night she approached me and said, "Let's start all over, okay?"

I said, "Okay." We hugged each other and smiled. No tension. No guilt.

As I looked into her eyes, I saw a different person. Her expression was beautiful. She looked as though she were starting life all over again with a new enthusiasm and an eagerness to learn what it was all about. She changed from a person whose feelings were easily hurt by the slightest comment to one who was hungry for information about where she needed to change. She wanted to see more and more reality any way she could. It was a joy to watch her eyes light up as people pointed out areas of wrongness that she might explore. It was as though she were on a treasure hunt, and each piece of information she discovered was another clue in her search for the reality she had missed.

I realized then how foolish I had been, because of my earlier fear, for not withdrawing support from the wrong action in our relationship.

After this change occurred, I stopped worrying about Betty. She stopped being jealous of my relationships with others and began developing many relationships with the people in the research group. I was thrilled.

Each new relationship was a delightful new surprise to her. She saw how restricted she had been to focus her attention on me.

We were experiencing a new kind of love for the first time. Not the love that holds one person in bondage to the other and restricts him from doing what the reality calls for, but the kind of love that gives a person the freedom to do what he should and to point out another's mistakes without encountering resistance. It is a love that gives a person the willingness to receive information because he wants to be in constant contact with reality.

I realize that I had had a misconception of love. I had thought that when you loved someone, you stood by him through thick and thin, no matter what. Now I see that real love is support for right action. If you really love a person, you will not support his wrong action and encourage him to do the same for you.

At one point I began asking her about those many months of tension-filled phone conversations. She said we didn't have to talk about it; we had both just been reasoning from misunderstandings. Why analyze a problem that no longer existed?

When the time arrived for her to leave, we said good-bye with no tears, no sense of loss. I didn't feel as though I had to hold on to her and restrict her from leaving. The reality was that it was time for her to go. With the new freedom we were experiencing, I felt just as close to her when we were apart as I did when we were together. I knew that our relationship was just there no matter how far apart we were in distance. Only the hooks had made it so painful for us to separate in the past.

When I spoke with her on the phone after she arrived home, the conversations were light and easy. What a contrast to the previous ones! She no longer pressured me to call her, and I didn't shake with fear that she might misunderstand.

When she returned for another visit about a year later, she said she felt as though she had never left. I felt the same way.

During this visit, I was heavily engaged in activities of the humanetics youth program. I often didn't come home until late, and a couple of times, I wondered if this would give her a problem. Then I realized that she wasn't like that anymore. Sometimes I almost had to shake myself into realizing how different the situation was. She wanted me to expand my activities and relationships. I felt the same way toward her.

During this period, we were involved in a writing program in which we wrote of our experiences with humanetics that might prove helpful for others.

Writing had been very difficult for Betty. She had formed a lot of wrong thinking from her childhood that had caused her to avoid any kind of writing. Even though she felt frightened of the idea of writing, she decided to do it anyway.

After she dove into the project, she was so excited about her change in attitude that she wanted to read me every page after she had finished with it. She found that she enjoyed the writing. Before her visit was finished, she told me she had written more in the last month than she had written in her entire lifetime.

When the change had taken place on her previous visit, she had talked about how wonderful it is just to respond to whatever happens instead of planning how your life should unfold and who should be involved in it. It was evident that she was dropping her personal plan and accepting the natural plan that reality offers—a plan in which all of life is laid out in front of a person. All he has to do is to take steps down the path that opens ahead, following right action wherever it leads.

While Betty and I were writing the articles about the changes that had occurred in our relationship, we began to talk about the tension that had developed so that we could accurately recount what had happened.

While we discussed these past situations, we both burst out laughing. We were laughing not because what had happened had been funny; it had been a tragedy. But after we had escaped from it, it no longer seemed like a tragedy—just crazy. It's crazy to use your emotions to control people and subject them to your will. And it's crazy to be afraid to withdraw support from what you know is wrong.

As I write, I find myself shedding a few tears from time to time, partly out of joy because these changes took place and partly out of the recognition of what our relationship would be like if these changes hadn't come.

If it weren't for the kids and their decision to support right action, the changes might never have occurred. They were the ones who provided courage and strength for doing what's right no matter what the cost. If it weren't for Mr. Wetherill's discovery of the law of absolute right, the kids would never have changed. It was humanetics that offered the only true escape from the hell that had engulfed our lives. And finally, if it weren't for the people who kept working toward proper understanding of the force of reality in human affairs, none of this would have been possible.

The world is filled with tragedies such as the one I have described. But this one found a happy ending.

Someday when humanetics is understood by everybody, all the tragedies on earth will be of the past, and the world will be filled with happy endings. With those happy endings, a new beginning will be born.

Games

FISH, WAR, Pinochle, Poker, Bridge. I learned them when I was about 8, 10, 16, 18 and 20 in that order. In each case I was passionate about them for years.

I haven't played any of them for some time now, or have I? There is a sense in which I have never completely stopped playing the games. The physical cards and formal playing rules are lacking, but how about the attitudes upon which the passion for playing is based?

The idea of a card game is to use your card resources and your own resourcefulness to gain the ultimate advantage over your opponent—victory with annihilation.

Only simplistic card games are open. Usually everybody hides his cards from others. We keep secrets in life games too, the better to take advantage. Sneaky peeks by an opponent bring out righteous indignation. How dare he deprive me of my secret advantages? If he knows I have aces, he will risk nothing I might take. If he knows I have deuces, he will crush me. We are not open and honest with each other in the game of life either, partly because we dare not, but primarily because we don't want to lose advantages.

FISH. I still remember how depressed I was when I lost practically every fish game on a rainy morning. I also remember how puffed up, proud and boastful I became when I won practically every game on a rainy morning. I thought I did it when I won and that it was my stupid little brother's incredible luck when I lost. The little jerk couldn't even remember what I had asked for previously. He just won by wild guessing. Sometimes he was holding foursies and didn't even know he had won. I had to tell him. It did not occur to me that the lay of the cards was pure chance. I wanted to win and then claim honors for the accomplishment.

When my brothers and our friends got a little older and could easily remember the fish requests, we developed cheat rules and played for nickels or other valuables such as baseball cards. We would deliberately fail to honor a request but at the risk of a challenge when we had to show our hand. If we had the requested cards, we automatically lost. If we had not cheated, the challenger automatically lost. Something like modern judicial and economic systems.

To confuse each other, we also made unwarranted requests hoping to mislead as to what we really wanted. The showdown rule was in force here also, making the whole thing perfectly "legal." Again, just like modern judicial and economic systems, immoral but OK. The bluffing eventually became so extreme it was no longer a reasonable game and certainly no fun.

It did not occur to me that cheating, even mutually agreeable legal cheating, is dishonest and destructive. I didn't even mind being cheated too much provided the punishments at the showdowns, be they card or life games, were sufficiently compensatory. That is pretty cruel thinking, but I called it justice.

Forty years later, 20 of them in the nonconflict research program of humanetics, I realized that cheating in life games is actually no fun either. It is life-destroying. It took the same amount of time to realize that punishment is a negative compensation, less than valueless, and no less destructive of the punisher than the punished.

WAR WAS fun because there was no real way to cheat if you and your opponent watched the reshuffles. Yet I still remember how passionate and excited I got when I had three of the four aces with the four kings, had my little brother down to wet eyes, and was under ten cards and going for that last ace and victory.

Whoever won would jump up and down and holler, "I won, I won!" taking full credit for the entire random distribution of the cards, which only a mathematician of the Creator's ability could have anticipated in advance.

I remember one game when I had all eight aces and all eight kings in a double deck game that had run all day. Yet the next day, my brother won it. I punched him good and felt somewhat better, but my father took offense at my attempts at justice, and shortly thereafter I didn't feel so good. I suffered because of the insanity of my rage at losing something that was never mine in the first place—the distribution of eight aces and kings in a double pack of cards shuffled many times. Once I had them, I thought them eternally mine to use for my personal advantage.

I stopped playing WAR long ago, but I didn't stop playing Creator. I took credit for anything I could get away with in the mistaken notion I was getting away with it. I have had the same attitude toward anything the Creator has seen fit to let me borrow and use a while. I assumed ownership and credit for anything from the size of my yard to my ability to think. I felt deprived when my so-called credits were withdrawn from me. I liked my aces. Everybody seems to. We cling to them until "death us do part."

A big lesson learned from the study of humanetics is this: The clinging to credits predisposes to the parting by death. No form of such insanity is compatible with survival.

PINOCHLE IS a more sophisticated game because the order of bidding and play can strongly compensate the random distribution of the cards. Reducing inevitable losses to a minimum was as much fun as winning maximally. In a sense, it was possible to win both ways.

Partner pinochle is even more sophisticated. Two hands in isolation, each with poor playing potential, can become quite powerful in combination. Odd-even and other bidding signals can assist winning the right to name trump. In this game the player is not alone. There's a partner to help.

The value of the alliance was often amazing to me, but what was done with that value? It should have illustrated the value of cooperation in all relationships. I only saw the false values of winning. Two against all was more advantageous for me than one against all.

My father and I became rather good at partnership pinochle. At a four-hour pinochle party, my father and I would invariably be high scorers. We were not at all appreciated by our opponents, however, who thought we were incredibly lucky. Often they would scream about each other's stupidity rather than admiring the skill of my father and me. Relationships became rather rueful when one of the opponents was my mother who issued no credit for skill at all. My father and I had bidding signals to let her win big every now and then. We feared she'd quit otherwise.

Some might say, "Pinochle is only a game. It's silly to behave like that." There are some people who do not behave like that playing card games. But we all do it in our little games of life. We indulge in sneaky secrets and sneaky conspiracies to win ourselves advantages that cause abominable relationships. I loved the pinochle battles. I kept a serious face but privately laughed and gloated as our opponents chewed each other out while losing. In the life game we use favors, or lack thereof, to hold our partners and opponents in line. Our trump cards are the threats of embarrassment or larger punishments.

It is interesting to note that all parties around the pinochle table would have described themselves as charitable, peace-loving civilized beings, whereas our behavior was more akin to Attila the Hun. The contrast is not exaggerated and shows the reasons for the actual state of human affairs as opposed to what it ought to be.

THEN I discovered poker. What a game! Conspiratorial, bluffing, combinational, mathematical, risky—all rolled together. It had all the best, or should I say the worst, features of the earlier card games and more. In my professional activities, I would directly compare the game of poker with the business environment, even while making speeches about the importance of cooperation and good business relationships. Neither I nor my listeners perceived the contradictions. It did not occur to me that poker and business games were essentially irrational and that I was a liar when I praised the benefits of cooperation I myself practiced only for advantage. Humanetics was needed to reveal that dishonesty.

Poker didn't remain attractive indefinitely. I discovered I had a bad face for bluffing. I was a darn good unconscious liar but a poor conscious one. I preferred to compete using truth instead of fiction. Besides, competing with truth was "honest" which, of course, I naturally thought I was. I got pretty good at penetrating the bluffs of others but couldn't mask my own effectively. The same situation seemed to exist in my career, placing a ceiling on how far I could go playing another game that kids call "King of the Mountain."

It is obvious that card games reflect life games. In card games we hide our insanities of purpose by saying, "It's only a game." In life itself there is no hiding the consequences. According to humanetics, all our troubles are due to dishonesty that causes insanity. I have grasped that dishonesty equates with insanity only because I have the theory of humanetics backed by the reference points of my own experience.

BRIDGE BECAME the next passion. I read all the bridge columns; I bought bridge textbooks; I bought play-yourself sets and took courses. Bridge seemed an ideal game to me, particularly contract bridge in which victory was related to how well I did with what I had rather than absolute score. My bridge face was as confusing in bridge as my poker face was transparent in poker. I was engaged in a partnership game making it possible to use another's strength to further the cause of victory, rather than being totally dependent on my own resources. In other words, it was possible to get an advantage by cooperation, the better to compete, disregarding the inherent immorality of taking advantage.

Like the horse-betting addict, who boasts only of his big-win days, I never much noticed that I lost far oftener than I won. The insane desire to win was so strong that I could tolerate many losses for one brief evening of glory.

I've run my life like a bridge game. It has brought me close to personal annihilation, the very thing I wished upon my card-playing or business opponents who obstructed my winning. In turn, when I have won, I have made many losers and pushed them toward their annihilation.

We are inattentive to the facts that there are always many more losers than winners and that all cannot be winners. To think so is equivalent to thinking that two objects can occupy the same place at the same time. Everybody knows that an attempt to occupy the space soon to be occupied by a two-ton automobile means death. Nobody seems aware that attempts to win may have exactly the same result, the only difference being that death may not be quite as instant.

And that, in summary, is what I am trying to point up. It is now clear to me that we are engaged in annihilating ourselves and each other, all the time thinking we are right—even noble—and, above all, quite clever. I have treated the game of life as if the sole objective were to have the best score or win all the chips in the house. The real purpose of life, I abandoned. The proper purpose is to use what I have been given to serve the purposes of the Prime Giver rather than my own.

Some, especially those thinking themselves "saved" or "called," may believe they already serve the purposes of the Prime Giver rather than their own purposes. In complete contradiction, I once thought so, even as I admitted to being a sinner. It has taken a thorough grounding, still ongoing, in the theory and practice of humanetics to realize how falsely I have imaged myself and then to revamp my thinking.

To my observation, there is zero evidence that without the availability of humanetics anybody could succeed in penetrating the very same image nor do I think it is probable.

What a tremendous relief it is to drop those useless, competitive objectives! But society still seems to worship the competitive person and deem competitive skills as constructive rather than destructive.

What a vastly different world this would be if we dropped our childish, dishonest, competitive and insane games of life and became truly civilized.